WALKS IN THE YORKSHIRE DALES

JACK KEIGHLEY'S

FAVOURITE ROUTES

CHURCH OF ST. MARY AND
ST. ALKELDA, MIDDLEHAM

WALK 43

WALKS IN THE YORKSHIRE DALES

JACK KEIGHLEY'S

★ **50** ★

FAVOURITE ROUTES

CICERONE

3

First published 2006, reprinted 2009 and 2014
Printed by KHL Printing, Singapore

This book updates and replaces the following three books, now out-of-print:
Walks in the Yorkshire Dales – ISBN 1 85284 054 X
Walks in the Yorkshire Dales Book 2 – ISBN 1 85284 065 X
Walks in the Yorkshire Dales Book 3 – ISBN 1 85284 085 X

Also by *Keighley*

WALKS IN LANCASHIRE WITCH COUNTRY
ISBN 1 85284 446 9

WALKS ON THE NORTH YORK MOORS
ISBN 1 85284 134 6

WALKS ON THE NORTH YORK MOORS BOOK TWO
ISBN 1 85284 197 4

FAMILY WALKS IN THE FOREST OF BOWLAND
ISBN 1 85284 251 2

WALKS IN RIBBLE COUNTRY
ISBN 1 85284 284 9

WALKS IN DALES COUNTRY
ISBN 1 85284 323 3

SOUTH PENNINE WALKS
ISBN 1 85284 390 X

INTRODUCTION

The area known as the Yorkshire Dales is many things to many people, but above all it is magnificent walking country. Walking has traditionally been the favourite pursuit of those visiting a region which offers a range of attractions perhaps unrivalled anywhere else in the whole of Britain :-

- wild, desolate fells
- extensive tracts of heather moorland
- rugged limestone scars, pavements and spectacular cliffs
- awe-inspiring potholes and caves
- deep river gorges and sparkling mountain streams
- exquisitely beautiful waterfalls
- green fertile valleys and flowery meadows
- outstanding views
- a vast network of public footpaths and bridleways
- remote, picturesque villages and bustling market towns
- ancient abbeys, churches and castles
- fascinating relics of former industries and ancient civilizations

The happiest person in the Dales must be the walker who is also a geologist. The major part of the area lies on a platform of ancient rocks – chiefly granite – known as the Askrigg Block. Apart from a few isolated exceptions, however, this base platform lies covered by strata of more recently formed rocks, and of these it is limestone which dominates the geology, and consequently the scenery, of the Yorkshire Dales.

The Great Scar Limestone is up to 400 feet thick in parts of the western and southern Dales, and is magnificently exposed in Ribblesdale, Wharfedale and Malhamdale. Here, above the glistening cliffs and scars, are vast areas of limestone pavements weathered from the exposed blocks of rock. About half the limestone pavement in Britain is found in the Yorkshire Dales. The Great Scar Limestone has not only undergone surface erosion, but is also honeycombed with complex underground cave systems. This is probably the finest caving area in Britain. The ordinary walker, who is too faint-hearted (or sensible?) to venture into these dank and sinister caverns, can safely sample the wonders of the underworld at three public show caves – White Scar Cave (Ingleton), Ingleborough Cave (Clapham) and Stump Cross Caverns (between Pateley Bridge and Grassington).

In the more northerly Dales, notably Wensleydale and Swaledale, the Great Scar Limestone lies hidden beneath layers of rock strata known as the Yoredale Series. Formed in an alternate succession of sandstone, shale and limestone (of a darker kind than the Great Scar variety), the Yoredales have weathered to produce hillsides with a distinctive stepped profile. In all parts of the Dales the highest fells are capped by beds of hard, coarse millstone grit.

Though nature has lavishly contributed this fine scenery, it is the influence of man which has helped to create the unique Dales landscape that we see today. The mineral resources

5

of the region have been exploited for many centuries. The Romans are known to have mined lead, and this industry developed until, at its peak in the nineteenth century, thousands of miners, chiefly in Swaledale and Wharfedale, were employed in extracting and processing lead. The ruins, levels, hushes and spoil heaps of these old mines still remain – stark and grim and desolate.

Since the discovery that grassland was improved by the application of burnt limestone (hence the profusion of old lime kilns), limestone working has developed into a major Dales industry, and today high quality limestone is quarried in several areas - most notably at Cracoe and Horton-in-Ribblesdale.

In the eighteenth century certain changes in the country's social and economic life had a marked effect on the Dales landscape. Between 1780 and 1820 successive Enclosure Acts led to a re-distribution of land and the construction of thousands of miles of drystone walls in the valleys and up the fellsides. This was an important building period in the Dales, and many of the present farms, cottages and barns are of that vintage. The Dales in fact have been inhabited since pre-history, and current walkers' paths date from earliest man to the drovers' and packhorse routes of the last two or three centuries. Many of these ancient green lanes still provide superb routes over the hills from dale to dale.

The other great influence on the landscape has been the grazing of sheep. The Dales are renowned for sheep, and years of careful breeding has produced animals which are ideally suited to the terrain and climate. Most popular is the famous black-faced 'Swaledale' with its curly horns. The Yorkshire Dales National Park Authority has chosen the Swaledale tup as its symbol. Sheep-grazing has a profound effect on the natural vegetation of the area.

My purpose in writing this introduction has been to attempt a general description of the superb countryside which the lucky user of this book may expect to enjoy, and the major factors which have shaped and fashioned it. My sincere wish is that you may derive as much pleasure from these walks as I have had in compiling them.

October 2005

ABOUT THIS BOOK

THE WALKS

All the walks described in this book are circular, and begin at a place where a car may be parked without causing an obstruction. They are fairly uniform in length, an average of about 6 miles making them half-day rather than full-day excursions. The routes, which adhere to public rights-of-way and permissive paths, should be free from serious difficulty and well within the capability of reasonably fit and agile walkers. Although the author has personally researched and walked all these routes, it must be pointed out that changes will occur quite frequently. Walkers may expect to encounter new stiles and fences and sometimes even diversions – either temporary or permanent. In such cases please note and obey all legitimate waymarks and signs.

NEITHER THE AUTHOR NOR THE PUBLISHER CAN ACCEPT RESPONSIBILITY FOR ANY ACCIDENT OR MISADVENTURE INCURRED ON THESE WALKS.

THE MAPS

The strip-maps show all relevant route-finding features, and great care has been taken to ensure accuracy, although for the sake of clarity there is deliberate distortion of scale in depicting routes along, for example, narrow lanes or through farmyards. In all maps north is at the top. In the ROUTE DIRECTIONS any mention of a stile, gate or footbridge means that it is used, unless otherwise stated. The maps and route directions together should suffice to make it quite clear to you how you've got lost. It is, however, strongly recommended that an Ordnance Survey map be carried, as this will add interest and enable the walker to identify distant features not mentioned in the text.

SYMBOLS USED ON THE MAPS

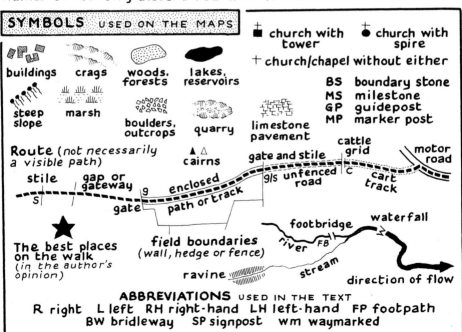

ABBREVIATIONS USED IN THE TEXT
R right   L left   RH right-hand   LH left-hand   FP footpath
BW bridleway   SP signpost   wm waymarked

WALKING IN THE DALES

★ Many of the routes in this book cross agricultural land, and farmers will not welcome inconsiderate visitors. When crossing fields keep closely to paths and walk in single file across hay meadows. Avoid climbing walls, and securely close all gates behind you (unless they are obviously meant to be left open).

★ Cars must not be parked where they obstruct field gates or cause damage to grass verges. Lock your car and securely hide from view any attractive or valuable articles (or take them with you).

★ Some of the walks described in this book cross high, exposed moorland terrain where the weather conditions may be less pleasant than at valley level. Should the weather turn nasty, don't hesitate to call it a day and return by the route along which you came.

★ Before setting out, let others know exactly where you are going. A mobile phone could be vital in an emergency.

★ When walking along a motor-road walk on the RIGHT to face oncoming traffic. The exception to this is on approaching a blind right-hand bend, when you should cross to the left for a clearer view.

CLOTHING AND EQUIPMENT

Boots or strong, comfortable shoes are essential (on the high moors and in winter BOOTS are the ONLY suitable footwear). A windproof jacket (preferably with a hood) will be needed. Thick, heavy sweaters are not a good idea – two or three lightweight layers are warmer and more adaptable to changing conditions. Denim is not at all suitable. In cold weather a woollen hat or cap will prevent the loss of a great deal of body heat. A rucksack is necessary. A small 'daysack' with a capacity of about 20-25 litres would be adequate for any of these walks. The author's rucksack will always contain the following items : –

● waterproof jacket and overtrousers ● small first aid kit ● spare laces ● large-scale O.S. map ● compass ● whistle ● plastic bottle for cold drink and/or flask for coffee or soup ● a high-calorie snack (e.g. chocolate or crisps) ● dog's drinking-water in a plastic bottle with either a 'cup-top' or a separate small bowl.

In wet, muddy conditions gaiters are an asset, once you've managed to get them on (it helps if you're a contortionist). A walking-stick is a matter of personal preference. Some walkers wouldn't be seen dead with one, but the author finds a knobstick useful for steep, slippery descents, fording streams, beating down nettles, discouraging aggressive animals and testing potentially boggy ground prior to sinking in up to the knees. The best knobsticks are made from hazel, ash or apple. Folding, or telescopic, metal jobs which are stuffable into a rucksack are currently popular, although they are a bit pricey.

CHILDREN

When taking children on country walks some thought must be given to distance and the type of terrain involved. Until you're sure of the child's capabilities, keep the distance short. Most of the walks in this book would probably be too much for a child under the age of five. As a rough rule-of-thumb, a child should be able to manage about a mile for each year of his age after his fifth birthday. Children should be warmly clothed and well-shod. One cannot always afford to buy expensive boots for growing feet, but at least the child should have strong shoes or close-fitting wellies. On no account should young children be allowed to wander off beyond the range of vision of responsible adults, and extreme care and control must be exercised in the vicinity of quarries, crags, potholes, old mine workings and ruined buildings.

DOGS

Though dogs are generally better-behaved than children they can nevertheless present certain difficulties which the owner should bear in mind. The two main problems are livestock and stiles - particularly ladder-stiles. Dogs must be kept under close control at all times, and MUST be on a lead in the proximity of farmyards and farm livestock. You will be lucky to complete any of these walks without encountering cattle and/or sheep. A lead should also be used when walking on motor-roads or on moorland during nesting-time (April-June). Some large, agile dogs are able to scramble over ladder-stiles, but small models need to be lifted over, and this can sometimes be rather awkward if you're walking alone. If your dog is big, fat and rheumaticky then you have problems. Best places for dogs are high, open ground and woodland; worst are motor-roads and lowland pastures. On very hot, sunny days dogs can become distressed, and may be at risk of heat-stroke. On summer walks the author has in his rucksack a small, plastic spray-bottle of water.

PLEASE OBSERVE THE

COUNTRY CODE

FASTEN ALL GATES

LEAVE NO LITTER

TAKE SPECIAL CARE ON COUNTRY ROADS

USE GATES AND STILES TO CROSS WALLS AND FENCES

ENJOY THE COUNTRYSIDE AND RESPECT ITS LIFE AND WORK

LEAVE LIVESTOCK, CROPS AND MACHINERY ALONE

GUARD AGAINST ALL RISK OF FIRE

PROTECT WILDLIFE, PLANTS AND TREES

HELP TO KEEP ALL WATER CLEAN

KEEP TO PUBLIC PATHS ACROSS FARMLAND

MAKE NO UNNECESSARY NOISE

KEEP YOUR DOG UNDER CLOSE CONTROL

THE WALKS

LOCATION MAP
SHOWING THE
STARTING POINTS
OF THE 50 WALKS DESCRIBED IN THIS BOOK

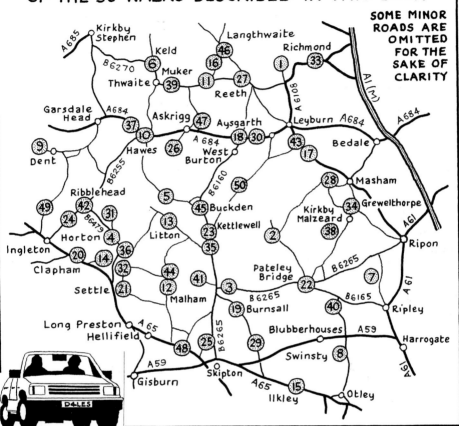

SOME MINOR
ROADS ARE
OMITTED
FOR THE
SAKE OF
CLARITY

The two maps OS EXPLORER OL 2 YORKSHIRE DALES SOUTHERN AND WESTERN AREAS and OS EXPLORER OL 30 YORKSHIRE DALES NORTHERN AND CENTRAL AREAS cover 36 of the 50 walks in this book.

OTHER MAPS REQUIRED

OS EXPLORER 26 NIDDERDALE Walks 2, 7, 22, 28, 34, 38, 40

OS EXPLORER 27 LOWER WHARFEDALE/WASHBURN VALLEY Walks 8, 15

OS EXPLORER OL19 HOWGILL FELLS Walks 9, 37

OS EXPLORER OL41 FOREST OF BOWLAND/RIBBLESDALE Walk 36

OS EXPLORER 302 NORTHALLERTON/THIRSK Walk 17

OS EXPLORER 304 DARLINGTON/RICHMOND Walk 33

1 MARSKE BECK

5½ MILES

P Marske, 4 miles W of Richmond. Parking space (honesty box) at W side of bridge.

Grid ref : 104 005

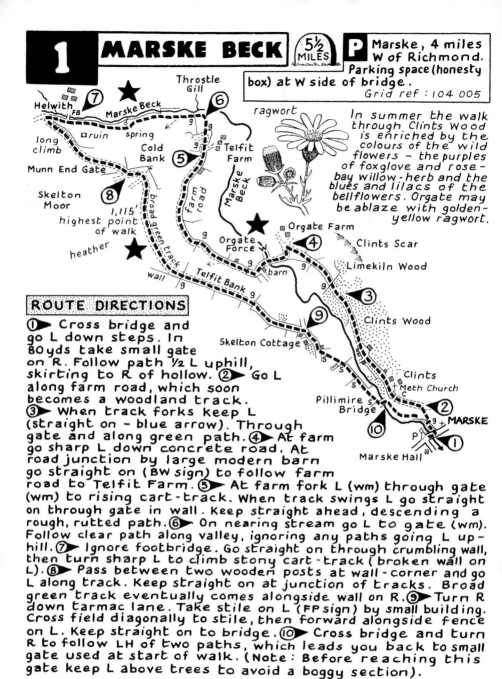

In summer the walk through Clints Wood is enriched by the colours of the wild flowers – the purples of foxglove and rose-bay willow-herb and the blues and lilacs of the bellflowers. Orgate may be ablaze with golden-yellow ragwort.

ROUTE DIRECTIONS

① Cross bridge and go L down steps. In 80yds take small gate on R. Follow path ½ L uphill, skirting to R of hollow. ② Go L along farm road, which soon becomes a woodland track. ③ When track forks keep L (straight on – blue arrow). Through gate and along green path. ④ At farm go sharp L down concrete road. At road junction by large modern barn go straight on (BW sign) to follow farm road to Telfit Farm. ⑤ At farm fork L (wm) through gate (wm) to rising cart-track. When track swings L go straight on through gate in wall. Keep straight ahead, descending a rough, rutted path. ⑥ On nearing stream go L to gate (wm). Follow clear path along valley, ignoring any paths going L uphill. ⑦ Ignore footbridge. Go straight on through crumbling wall, then turn sharp L to climb stony cart-track (broken wall on L). ⑧ Pass between two wooden posts at wall-corner and go L along track. Keep straight on at junction of tracks. Broad green track eventually comes alongside wall on R. ⑨ Turn R down tarmac lane. Take stile on L (FP sign) by small building. Cross field diagonally to stile, then forward alongside fence on L. Keep straight on to bridge. ⑩ Cross bridge and turn R to follow LH of two paths, which leads you back to small gate used at start of walk. (Note: Before reaching this gate keep L above trees to avoid a boggy section).

MARSKE HALL is not passed on the walk, but its elegant Georgian facade can be seen from just along the Leyburn road. It was the home of the Hutton family from the late 16th C. until recently, but is now converted into flats. Matthew Hutton was Archbishop of York 1595-1606, and a later Matthew, having also been Archbishop of York, became Archbishop of Canterbury in 1757.

THE EXQUISITE VALLEY OF MARSKE BECK, ALTHOUGH NOT LARGE ENOUGH TO BE REGARDED AS A SEPARATE DALE, IS A MICROCOSM OF SWALEDALE ITSELF. FROM THE SUPERB GREEN TRACK ALONG THE TOP OF TELFIT BANK THE SCENE FAR BELOW IS ONE OF SYLVAN BEAUTY, WITH THE SPARKLING BECK WINDING ITS WAY THROUGH WOODS AND MEADOWS BELOW A SPLENDID LIMESTONE EDGE. THERE'S A LONG, STEADY CLIMB FROM HELWITH TO MUNN END GATE; ALL THE REST IS EASY WALKING.

1

This village, which stands in delightful surroundings on the very edge of the National Park, is well-kept and has a decidedly affluent air. In Norman days it belonged to the Constable of Richmond Castle. The BRIDGE, from where our walk begins, has ribbed arches of the 15th C. The CHURCH is dedicated to the Saxon St. Edmund, and dates in part from c1090. The S doorway is Norman, and there is also a blocked N doorway of similar vintage. The octagonal font is dated 1663. The church was extensively rebuilt in 1683, and further restoration took place in 1830 and 1889. St. Edmund's has registers going back as far as 1597. A visit to this interesting and unusual church is a must, and requires only a very short detour uphill from the bridge.

ORGATE FORCE, a picturesque waterfall, is very impressive after heavy rain. It's on private land and, despite a well-trodden path along the RH side of the beck, has no public access.

Note this old waterwheel near Pillimire Bridge

THE FAMOUS **SWALEDALE SHEEP** CAN USUALLY BE SEEN IN LARGE FLOCKS IN THE VICINITY OF HELWITH. IT CAN BE RECOGNIZED BY ITS BLACK FACE WITH WHITE SNOUT. IT IS A TOUGH AND HARDY CREATURE WELL ABLE TO SURVIVE HARSH WINTERS ON THE HIGHEST MOORLAND GRAZING. THE COARSE WOOL IS IDEAL FOR CARPET-MAKING. THE SWALEDALE CROSSES WELL WITH OTHER BREEDS.

MAP O.S. Explorer OL 30 Yorkshire Dales Northern and Central areas.

2 CAVES & GORGES OF NIDDERDALE

6½ MILES

P How Stean. Car park *(honesty box)* at foot of gorge, opposite a row of garages.

Grid ref: 097 733
If this is full, there is a large car park in the field behind the cafe. There is also a car park at Middlesmoor, at top end of village

ROUTE DIRECTIONS

① Go L up tarmac lane. After visiting How Stean Gorge continue up lane. ② Turn sharp R (FP Middlesmoor). Follow path down to footbridge and up to gate. Turn L to wall-stile and follow clear path upstream. It eventually climbs to stile at top of wood. ③ To visit How Stean Force keep straight on, soon forking L to follow clear path across large hollow. Return to stile, but take another one to its L. Climb diagonally R to gap in fence, then turn R (wm) to stile at bottom end of wall. Straight on to stile, then bear slightly L up to gap in crosswall. Head for farm. ④ On reaching gate turn L (wm). At top of field take gate (wm) on R and descend to Meth. Church. Go L up through village. ⑤ Just before reaching car park take fence-stile on R. Pass corner of car park and LH end of plantation. Turn R towards farm and follow path through four stiles to walled lane. Go R along it. ⑥ At plantation take gate (wm) on R and drop steeply to stile at far corner. Head towards farm (line of stiles). ⑦ Go L along tarmac road. 150 yds past bridge take gate on R and descend to Goyden Pot. Follow stream bed (keep on LH side of fence) and on upstream. ⑧ Cross footbridge and return downstream (slippery path). Ford tributary stream and turn L past barn to climb steeply. Turn R along farm road. ⑨ Pass R of house. At far end of garden take RH of two gates (wm). Follow waymarks to zig-zag down. Cross dry stream bed, through farmyard and out along access road. ⑩ When it turns R go straight on through gate/stile (wm). Keep L to follow wm path alongside dry river bed. At gate cross river bed (Dry Wath) and follow clear path down valley. ⑪ Go R down road into Lofthouse. Turn sharp R at drinking fountain. Cross footbridge, then road, and forward past cricket field. Bear slightly R to gate, then straight on along road.

HOW STEAN FORCE, a wide, low waterfall, is impressive only after heavy rain. Often it's completely dry.

MH = Manchester Hole
GP = Goyden Pot

14

👣 A WALK OF EXQUISITE CHARM AND INFINITE VARIETY WHICH BEGINS AT THE SPECTACULAR GORGE OF HOW STEAN. THE WALKER WILL ENJOY IDYLLIC RIVER SCENERY AND SUPERB VIEWS OF UPPER NIDDERDALE. THE ROUTE VISITS THE FAMOUS CAVES OF GOYDEN POT AND MANCHESTER HOLE, AND ENDS WITH A STROLL ALONG A DELIGHTFUL GREEN LANE.

2

❗ The ford just beyond point 8 can be awkward when the stream's in spate. To avoid this section you could go directly from point 7 to point 10, using the access road to the R of Limley Farm. This would reduce the walk to 4¾ miles. Another option would be to proceed as far as Manchester Hole, then return to points 7 and 10.

HOW STEAN GORGE

provides a dramatic natural spectacle. This limestone ravine is 70' deep in places, with rocky footpaths winding their way along the sides and over slender footbridges. **TOM TAYLOR'S CAVE** runs for 170 yds from the gorge to the field behind the café, and can be easily negotiated with the aid of a torch. It is reputed to have been the hiding place of a local highwayman. A visit to How Stean is a very special day out.

★

HOW STEAN TUNNEL is a 56 yd long cave carrying a stream under the road.

Look out for the **ROE DEER**, particularly in the vicinity of How Stean Force. This shy little deer (only 2' high) is not often seen, but you may hear its alarm call – a short, sharp, dog-like bark.

MIDDLESMOOR

, A VILLAGE OF FASCINATING ALLEYWAYS, STANDS ON A HILLSIDE AT ALMOST 1000' ABOVE SEA-LEVEL. FROM THE CHURCHYARD THERE IS A MAGNIFICENT VIEW DOWN THE VALLEY TOWARDS THE DISTANT GOUTHWAITE RESERVOIR.

The Water Authority road which we meet at point 7 follows the line of the **NIDD VALLEY LIGHT RAILWAY**, which ran from Pateley Bridge up to the reservoir construction sites at Angram and Scar House. The railway was owned by Bradford Corporation, and the loco illustrated – 'Gadie' – was named after the Lord Mayor of that city. The line operated from 1907 to 1937.

GOYDEN POT AND MANCHESTER HOLE

GOYDEN POT is a complex river cave through which the Nidd flows for more than 2 miles before surfacing below Lofthouse.

In normal weather, when the river bed is dry, the large

Goyden Pot

entrance chamber can be explored, but take a good torch. The chamber ends at a triple junction, which is as far as many will wish to go. The RH branch leads down to the river. Any further exploration should be left to the expert. About 300 yds upstream the Nidd sinks underground

at MANCHESTER HOLE. There is a large entrance hole a few yards above the river bank with an easy descent of some 20' to the river passage.

The church-like building on the skyline is really a shooting-hut.

GOYDEN POT MUST NOT BE ENTERED IF ANY WATER IS FLOWING INTO IT.

| MAP | O.S. Explorer 26 Nidderdale |

3 CONISTONE DIB & DIB SCAR

6½ MILES

P Grassington. Large car park (pay and display) at the National Park Centre, off Hebden Road at S end of village.
Grid ref: 002 637

As an alternative you could omit Grassington by parking at Conistone (space for about 4 cars opposite the Methodist Chapel)

ROUTE DIRECTIONS

① Walk up through village. At top of Main Street go L along Chapel Street. ② Go R up Bank Lane to its end at gate/stile. Continue up narrow field, keeping alongside its RH wall. From stile bear R (FP sign) to ladder-stile and maintain direction along clear path. ③ Over ladder-stile take LH of two paths. At circular walled enclosure path forks - keep R. ④ From gate at Bare House take path bearing slightly L. Drop to pass R of copse. Follow clear path, heading towards distant mast. ⑤ From stile in crosswall there's a choice. For full walk take RH path (FP Kettlewell). For short cut bear L down obvious depression. ⑥ At head of valley take ladder-stile on L. Descend rocky gully - CARE NEEDED - to another ladder-stile. Continue down valley to Conistone. ⑦ At tarmac road go L (SP Grassington 3). Turn L (FP Grassington 2½) up rough lane. Ignoring any paths branching L, follow cart-track, which eventually becomes a broad, green path. It passes through two gates at wall-corners, then swings L (wm) to climb LH side of valley. ⑧ Cross stile (FP sign) to rising path beyond shallow valley. ⑨ Take ladder-stile on L and turn R. Keep roughly parallel with wall on R to reach stile in crosswall. ⑩ Forward to another stile, then keep L across field to narrow slit-stile. ⑪ At end of next field cross stile and turn L (FP sign). Take stile on R (FP sign) and straight across field to gate into Bank Lane. Turn R to retrace outward route.

(map labels:) mast, Conistone Dib, Gurling Trough, Bull Scar, Dales Way, kiln, outcrops and boulders, Back Pasture, copse, trough, Bare House, CONISTONE, cart track, barn, GP, walled enclosure, Dib Scar, Look R to see perched boulders on skyline, Lea Green, ruin, awkward, Bastow Wood, fat man's agony, Bank Lane, GRASSINGTON, Nat. Park Centre car park, Hebden

There are no hedges or fences on this map. All the field boundaries are WALLS.

16

THIS OUTSTANDING WALK TAKES IN SOME OF WHARFEDALE'S FINEST LIMESTONE SCENERY. CONISTONE DIB IS A SUPERB DRY VALLEY WITH SAVAGELY IMPRESSIVE ROCK SCENERY AT ITS HEAD AND FOOT. DIB SCAR, MORE WOODED IN CHARACTER, IS NEGOTIATED BY A SPLENDID HIGH-LEVEL PATH. GOOD, CLEAR PATHS THROUGHOUT, BUT LOTS OF STILES - SOME OF WHICH ARE A BIT AWKWARD.

! *The initial descent of Conistone Dib, from point 6, is steep, rocky and slippery. You can avoid this by using the short cut from point 5, but you'll miss some of the walk's most dramatic scenery.*

GRASSINGTON

the undisputed capital of Upper Wharfedale is one of the best-loved villages in the Dales. Granted a market charter in 1282, Grassington endured some troubled times in the 14th C, when Scottish raiders were

BARE HOUSE (locally pronounced 'Barrass') is a lonely, remote and long-abandoned farmhouse.

frequent visitors and the Black Death wiped out a quarter of the population. In the early 1800s the village was the base for the Grassington Moor lead-mining field, when up to 600 men were employed in the then thriving industry. Now tourism is all-important, and Grassington has pubs, cafés and shops in profusion grouped around its picturesque cobbled square. It's always busy, and at weekend EXTREMELY busy.

Limekiln just beyond Bare House.

CONISTONE DIB IS A CLASSIC EXAMPLE OF A DRY LIMESTONE VALLEY. AT ITS FOOT THE VALLEY NARROWS TO BECOME A SPECTACULAR ROCKY GORGE (GURLING TROUGH) WITH VERTICAL WALLS AT ONE POINT ONLY ABOUT 4' APART. THE VIEW FROM THE HEAD OF THE DIB (POINT 6) IS AWESOME.

St. Mary's Church

CONISTONE is a pretty little village bypassed by the main valley road. Its focal point is a tiny green, on which stands a lofty maypole. The CHURCH OF ST. MARY is one of the oldest in Craven. Two pre-Norman arches survive; others are Early English. Just inside the churchyard is a memorial to 6 young cavers who died when the nearby Mossdale Caverns flooded in 1967. Some of Conistone's farmhouses and barns are of the late 17th C — you may notice a blocked doorway inscribed 'IT 1697'. Note also the dovecot built into the wall of a barn. Several barns have been converted into private residences.

DIB SCAR, WHICH IS OFTEN DESCRIBED AS A MINIATURE MALHAM COVE, IS MORE WOODED THAN CONISTONE DIB. ICE-AGE MELTWATERS CARVED OUT A GORGE HERE, RIMMED BY CLIFFS WHICH WOULD ONCE HAVE HAD A WATERFALL SOME 70' HIGH.

MAP O.S. Explorer OL 2 Yorkshire Dales Southern and Western areas.

4 PENYGHENT

P Horton in Ribblesdale. Car park (Pay and display) at north end of village.
Grid ref: 807 726

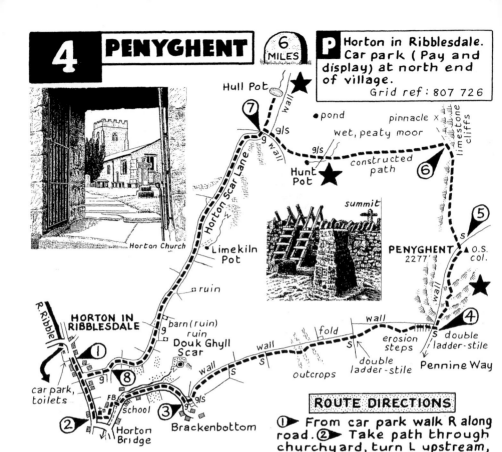

Horton Church

Hull Pot

pond

pinnacle X

wet, peaty moor

limestone cliffs

gls

g wall

Horton Scar Lane

constructed path

Hunt Pot

summit

PENYGHENT 2277'

O.S. col.

Limekiln Pot

ruin

HORTON IN RIBBLESDALE

barn (ruin) ruin

Douk Ghyll Scar

R. Ribble

car park, toilets

FB

school

Horton Bridge

Brackenbottom

fold

wall

wall

wall

erosion steps

double ladder-stile

double ladder-stile

outcrops

Pennine Way

ROUTE DIRECTIONS

① From car park walk R along road. ② Take path through churchyard, turn L upstream, cross footbridge and go L past school and on up lane. ③ Take gate on L (SP Penyghent Summit). Through gate/stile and turn L (FP sign) to begin long climb by wall. ④ At stile on ridge turn L to ascend steep, rocky path to summit. ⑤ Cross ladder-stile and go straight ahead on broad path, which initially heads in the direction of the prominent crater of Hull Pot before veering R to descend gently. ⑥ At foot of limestone cliffs turn L (SP Horton in Ribblesdale) down clear path. Just after crossing a wall detour 50 yds L to view Hunt Pot. ⑦ At gate on L (BW Horton in R 1½) turn R to make short detour to Hull Pot. Return to gate and walk down walled track. ⑧ Keep R at fork.

HUNT POT AND HULL POT

Hunt Pot

These notable potholes differ vastly in appearance. HUNT POT is a narrow slit, 200' deep and engulfing a stream. In its attractive setting it is a classic pothole entrance. Slippery rocks make a close approach highly dangerous. HULL POT is an immense crater 300' long, 60' wide and 60' deep. In very wet weather a beck plunges over the northern lip in a spectacular waterfall before sinking into the crater's bouldery floor.

PENYGHENT IS ONE OF THE FEW DALES MOUNTAINS WHICH ACTUALLY *LOOKS* LIKE A MOUNTAIN, AND ITS CHALLENGING PROFILE DRAWS WALKERS LIKE A MAGNET. THIS IS NOT A PRETTY WALK, FOR THE SURROUNDING MOORS ARE BLEAK AND DESOLATE, BUT, BY WAY OF COMPENSATION, THERE IS A SUCCESSION OF IMPRESSIVE NATURAL FEATURES ALONG THE WAY. THE WALK IS ON CLEAR PATHS THROUGHOUT, BUT IS STRENUOUS, WITH A CLIMB OF 1,400' — STEEP AND ROCKY IN PLACES — FROM BRACKENBOTTOM TO THE SUMMIT.

4

HORTON IN RIBBLESDALE

is not in itself particularly attractive, but is a fine centre for walking and caving. The long, straggling village has the look of being two separate communities set about half a mile apart. At the S end of the village the Golden Lion faces the rugged old church . The Golden Lion was an outdoor education centre for 18 years before reverting to a pub in 1988. The church dates back at least to the reign of Henry I (1100 - 35) and, though much of the present building is of late 14th/early 15th C vintage, the nave arcades, font and S doorway have survived from the original Norman church. The W window has panels depicting Thomas à Becket and the coat-of-arms of Jervaulx Abbey. Horton's old character was largely destroyed in late Victorian times with the building of unprepossessing housing for railway and quarry workers.

— •◆• —

THE PENNINE WAY is a 270 mile route for masochistic walkers, its termini being Edale, in Derbyshire, and Kirk Yetholm, in Scotland's border country. Wayfarers who have started at Edale, as most do, will limp into Horton's famous Pen-y-Ghent Café having completed about 92 miles of their journey.

Penyghent from the first double ladder-stile

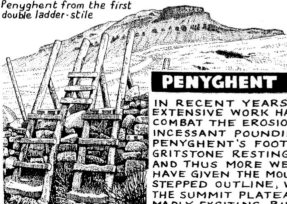

PENYGHENT

IN RECENT YEARS EXTENSIVE WORK HAS BEEN NECESSARY TO COMBAT THE EROSION CAUSED BY THE INCESSANT POUNDING OF BOOTS ON PENYGHENT'S FOOTPATHS. BANDS OF HARD GRITSTONE RESTING ON BEDS OF SOFTER, AND THUS MORE WEATHERWORN, LIMESTONE HAVE GIVEN THE MOUNTAIN ITS DISTINCTIVE STEPPED OUTLINE, WITH 90' CRAGS FRINGING THE SUMMIT PLATEAU. THE SUMMIT IS NOT MADLY EXCITING, BUT THE GLORIOUS VIEW TAKES IN PENDLE HILL, THE BOWLAND FELLS, MOST OF THE DALES, MORECAMBE BAY AND SOUTH LAKELAND.

MAP O.S. Explorer OL 2 Yorkshire Dales Southern and Western areas.

section of the Buckden-Hawes road just above Yockenthwaite Bridge, where the road runs beside the River Wharfe.

Grid ref: 900 794

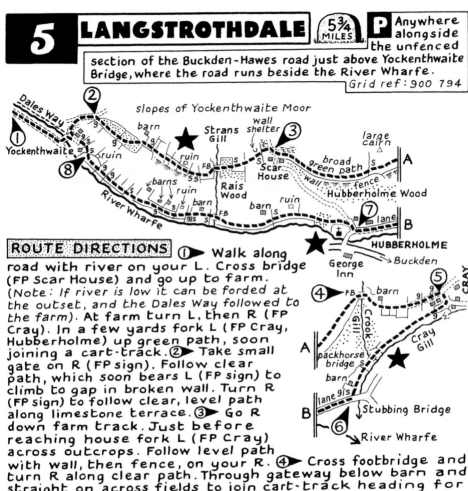

ROUTE DIRECTIONS

① Walk along road with river on your L. Cross bridge (FP Scar House) and go up to farm. (Note: If river is low it can be forded at the outset, and the Dales Way followed to the farm). At farm turn L, then R (FP Cray). In a few yards fork R (FP Cray, Hubberholme) up green path, soon joining a cart-track. ② Take small gate on R (FP sign). Follow clear path, which soon bears L (FP sign) to climb to gap in broken wall. Turn R (FP sign) to follow clear, level path along limestone terrace. ③ Go R down farm track. Just before reaching house fork L (FP Cray) across outcrops. Follow level path with wall, then fence, on your R. ④ Cross footbridge and turn R along clear path. Through gateway below barn and straight on across fields to join cart-track heading for buildings. ⑤ Immediately past second building on R turn sharp R (FP sign) down walled track to gate. (Note: To visit pub at Cray, keep straight on at point 5, along the LH track). From gate go forward along clear path, soon descending steeply to follow stream. ⑥ Go R along tarmac lane. ⑦ Just before church turn R (Dales Way FP) along farm road. Follow church-yard wall (FP Yockenthwaite) and continue along 'made' path. Path is obvious almost throughout — if in doubt keep close to river. ⑧ Approaching farm take gated stile up on R. Go forward to fence-stile, then through gate to join farm road down to bridge and road.

By using the farm road linking Hubberholme and Scar House, the route can be conveniently adapted into two separate short walks, viz: —

a) YOCKENTHWAITE – SCAR HOUSE – HUBBERHOLME – YOCKENTHWAITE 3½ MILES

b) HUBBERHOLME (Space to park by the river) – SCAR HOUSE – CRAY – HUBBERHOLME 2¾ MILES

THERE CAN BE FEW WALKS WHICH OFFER SUCH GENEROUS REWARDS FOR SUCH LITTLE EFFORT. THE OUTWARD HALF TRAVERSES A LEVEL LIMESTONE LEDGE - AN ENCHANTING BALCONY HIGH ABOVE THE FLOOR OF LOVELY LANGSTROTHDALE. THE DESCENT IS BY CRAY GILL, A DELIGHTFUL STREAM WITH WATERFALLS, CASCADES AND TINY GORGES, AND THE RETURN IS ALONGSIDE THE WHARFE AND SOME SUPERB RIVER SCENERY. TO PILE RICHES UPON RICHES, THERE ARE ALSO TWO EXCELLENT PUBS ALONG THE WAY. EASY WALKING. CLEAR PATHS THROUGHOUT.

5

LANGSTROTHDALE

is the name given to Upper Wharfedale above Buckden. In Norman times it was a hunting chase for deer and game. YOCKENTHWAITE, a fine example of a Georgian farmhouse, was probably built in the mid-18th C.

The graceful bridge at Yockenthwaite

STRANS GILL

A footbridge crosses a deep, dry, narrow limestone gully, beneath which is an extensive cave system accessible to only the most expert potholers. A section known as the 'Passage of Time' is considered one of the most beautiful caves in England.

SCAR HOUSE has a stone over its door dated 1698, but the house is certainly older than that. It was at one time used as a Quaker meeting house.

HUBBERHOLME

THE PRIDE OF THIS VILLAGE IS THE LOVELY 12th C. CHURCH, WHICH IS NOW DEDICATED TO ST. MICHAEL AND ALL ANGELS, THOUGH DURING ITS LONG HISTORY IT HAS BEEN KNOWN ALSO AS ST. OSWALD'S AND ST. LEONARD'S. THE SUPERBLY CARVED OAK ROOD LOFT DATES FROM 1558, AND IS ONE OF THE VERY FEW TO HAVE ESCAPED THE EDICT OF

CRAY is a tiny hamlet over 1000' above sea-level. It is the last outpost in Wharfedale on the B6160 road over Kidstones Pass to Bishopdale and Wensleydale. The **WHITE LION** is a fine hostelry with a wide selection of ales and good food. On the descent alongside the immensely attractive **CRAY GILL** note the charming little stone bridge, which is thought to have been on a packhorse route from Settle to Askrigg.

ELIZABETH I THAT ALL SUCH STRUCTURES SHOULD BE DESTROYED. ALSO OF GREAT ANTIQUITY IS THE HEAVY, STUDDED DOOR IN THE S PORCH. THE PEWS AND CHOIR STALLS WERE MADE IN 1934 BY ROBERT THOMPSON OF KILBURN, AND BEAR HIS TRADEMARK MOUSE. JUST ACROSS THE BRIDGE STANDS THE GEORGE INN, WHICH WAS ONCE THE VICARAGE. HERE IS HELD AN ANNUAL NEW YEAR AUCTION, WHEN A NEARBY FIELD (THE POOR PASTURE) IS LET OUT FOR GRAZING TO THE HIGHEST BIDDER. THE CUSTOM IS NEARLY 1000 YEARS OLD, AND THE PROCEEDS ARE USED TO HELP THE OLD FOLK OF THE PARISH. THE GEORGE WAS MUCH-FREQUENTED BY THE FAMOUS AUTHOR J. B. PRIESTLEY, WHOSE GRAVE IS IN THE NEARBY CHURCHYARD. THE BRIDGE WAS RECORDED AS BEING IN RUINS IN 1709, AND WAS REBUILT IN 1734.

MAP O.S. Explorer OL 30 Yorkshire Dales Northern and Central areas.

6 KISDON & THE SWALE GORGE

5½ MILES

P Keld. Large car park (honesty box) at bottom end of village. Grid ref: 892 012

ROUTE DIRECTIONS ① Walk up through village, keeping L at fork. Continue forward along main road. ② At barn go L (BW Muker 2) down walled track. Cross slab bridge and follow stony track uphill. Keep straight ahead as it becomes a broad green path, passing through a series of gates and eventually descending towards Muker. ③ At a Pennine Way sign bear L to descend walled track. ④ Follow farm road zig-zagging down to village. ⑤ At the village bear L, then turn L at Post Office (SP Gunnerside, Keld). Follow flagged path through meadows. On reaching river turn R (FP Gunnerside) to cross big footbridge, then go L (FP Keld) along stony vehicle track. ⑥ At lead mine ruins cross footbridge and go forward through gate to follow broad, rising track. ⑦ After crossing a bridge fork L (PW Keld) down clear path to cross footbridge. Climb broad track and at junction go R.

KELD
car park, toilets
B 6270
① ⑦ East Gill Force
Beldi Hill
ruin gls
Hope House FB
② Kisdon Force (heard but not seen)
FB
barn
rough track
gradient eases
cottage
▲ KISDON 1636'
superb green bridleway
wall
Hooker Mill Scar
x SP Muker
pen
corpse road
Thwaite Stones
PW sign
PW
Kisdon Cottage
③
farm road
④
⑤
MUKER
flagged path
gls

old tractor
Crackpot Hall
barn
Swinner Gill
ruins
FB ⑥

The name 'Crackpot Hall' did not refer to the mental state of its occupants. 'Crackpot' means 'pothole of the crows'

R. Swale
broad vehicle track
Arngill Force (slender waterfall)
Rampsholme Bridge

CRACKPOT HALL was abandoned in 1953 because of subsidence caused by lead-mining.

The rusting remains of an old tractor near Crackpot Hall.

☠ The 'CORPSE ROAD' was a medieval funeral track from Keld to the (then) nearest church at Grinton, 12 miles down the dale.

HOPE HOUSE used to be a pub. The **CATHOLE INN** as it was called, was bought in 1954 by two teetotal brothers, who converted it into a private residence.

22

A CLASSIC WALK IN THE MOST SPECTACULARLY BEAUTIFUL PART OF SWALEDALE. FROM KELD THE GREEN 'CORPSE ROAD' GIVES SUPERB VIEWS DOWN THE DALE, WHILST THE RETURN FROM MUKER IS A COMPLETE CONTRAST - A STONY RIVERSIDE TRACK LEADING PAST EVOCATIVE LEAD-MINING RUINS TO THE DRAMATIC SCENERY OF A LIMESTONE GORGE. VERY CLEAR PATHS THROUGHOUT - IT WOULD TAKE A GENIUS TO GET LOST ON THIS ONE.

6

KELD

This tiny, haphazard cluster of grey buildings – Swaledale's upper-most settlement - has its roots in Viking times, and in the Middle Ages was called Appletreekeld. 'Keld' is Old Norse for 'spring' or 'well'. Day-walkers flock here in droves, and footsore Pennine Way and Coast-to-Coast pilgrims recharge their batteries at the popular Youth Hostel. The lure of Keld is the rushing river with its series of attractive falls and cataracts. Wain Wath Force, Catrake Force, Kisdon Force and East Gill Force are all close by, although the latter, on a small tributary stream, is the only one seen on this particular walk.

East Gill Force

KISDON

This steep-sided hill is a geological freak. Prior to the ice-age of some 13,000 years ago the Swale flowed down the valley on the west side of the hill. Ice-movements, however, caused this valley to become blocked by glacial boulder-clay, and the river cut a new course – the present gorge – leaving Kisdon isolated in the middle.

Looking back to Kisdon Cottage, a house with a wonderful view.

SWINNER GILL

THIS AWESOME, CRAG-LINED RAVINE WAS ONCE A FLOURISHING LEAD-MINING CENTRE. THE INDUSTRY DIED OUT IN THE LATE 19THC, LEAVING A SCENE OF WIDESPREAD DEVASTATION, AND SCARS THAT NATURE HAS NOT YET MANAGED TO HEAL. THE RUINED SMELT MILL WORKED FROM 1769 TO c 1820. IT HAD TWO ROOMS. THE RH ROOM (AS SEEN FACING THE RUIN WITH YOUR BACK TO THE STREAM) HOUSED THE SMELTING HEARTHS. IN THE LH ROOM WERE THE BELLOWS, DRIVEN BY A WATERWHEEL. VISIBLE BEHIND THE MILL ARE THE REMAINS OF A 'FLUE', WHICH CARRIED FUMES UP ONTO THE MOOR.

Note this old lead-miners' bridge at the foot of Beldi Hill.

FOR SOME NOTES ON MUKER PLEASE REFER TO WALK 39

MAP O.S. Explorer OL 30 Yorkshire Dales Northern and Central areas.

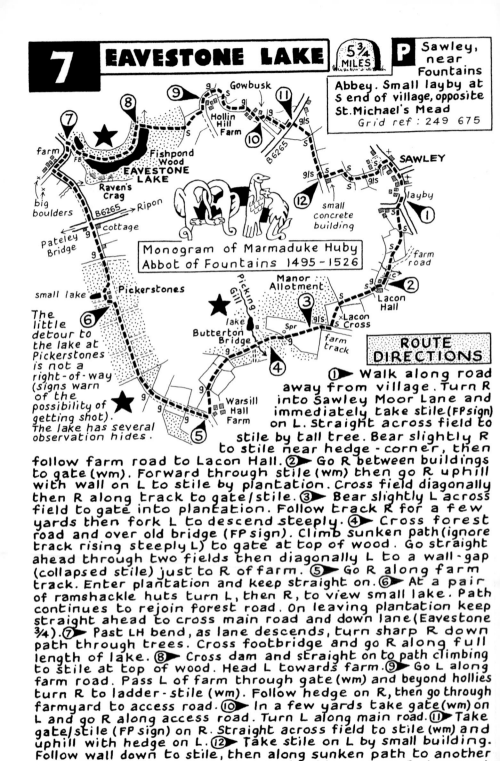

7 EAVESTONE LAKE

5¾ MILES

P Sawley, near Fountains Abbey. Small layby at S end of village, opposite St. Michael's Mead
Grid ref : 249 675

Gowbusk
Hollin Hill Farm
B6265
SAWLEY
layby
farm
FB
Fishpond Wood
EAVESTONE LAKE
Raven's Crag
big boulders
B6265 → Ripon
cottage
Pateley Bridge
small lake
Pickerstones
Picking Gill
Manor Allotment
lake
Butterton Bridge
Spr
Lacon Cross
farm track
Lacon Hall
small concrete building
Warsill Hall Farm

Monogram of Marmaduke Huby
Abbot of Fountains 1495–1526

The little detour to the lake at Pickerstones is not a right-of-way (signs warn of the possibility of getting shot). The lake has several observation hides.

ROUTE DIRECTIONS

① Walk along road away from village. Turn R into Sawley Moor Lane and immediately take stile (FP sign) on L. Straight across field to stile by tall tree. Bear slightly R to stile near hedge-corner, then follow farm road to Lacon Hall. ② Go R between buildings to gate (wm). Forward through stile (wm) then go R uphill with wall on L to stile by plantation. Cross field diagonally then R along track to gate/stile. ③ Bear slightly L across field to gate into plantation. Follow track R for a few yards then fork L to descend steeply. ④ Cross forest road and over old bridge (FP sign). Climb sunken path (ignore track rising steeply L) to gate at top of wood. Go straight ahead through two fields then diagonally L to a wall-gap (collapsed stile) just to R of farm. ⑤ Go R along farm track. Enter plantation and keep straight on. ⑥ At a pair of ramshackle huts turn L, then R, to view small lake. Path continues to rejoin forest road. On leaving plantation keep straight ahead to cross main road and down lane (Eavestone ¾). ⑦ Past LH bend, as lane descends, turn sharp R down path through trees. Cross footbridge and go R along full length of lake. ⑧ Cross dam and straight on to path climbing to stile at top of wood. Head L towards farm. ⑨ Go L along farm road. Pass L of farm through gate (wm) and beyond hollies turn R to ladder-stile (wm). Follow hedge on R, then go through farmyard to access road. ⑩ In a few yards take gate (wm) on L and go R along access road. Turn L along main road. ⑪ Take gate/stile (FP sign) on R. Straight across field to stile (wm) and uphill with hedge on L. ⑫ Take stile on L by small building. Follow wall down to stile, then along sunken path to another stile. Follow hedge on L to emerge onto village green. R along road.

ON THE EASTERN FRINGES OF THE DALES, BETWEEN PATELEY BRIDGE, RIPON AND MASHAM, CAN BE FOUND SOME OF THE LOVELIEST AND MOST PEACEFUL COUNTRYSIDE IN YORKSHIRE. THIS WALK, TYPICAL OF THE AREA, IS AN EXQUISITE BLEND OF GENTLE, ROLLING PASTURES, BEAUTIFUL WOODLAND, CHARMING LAKES AND WONDERFULLY EXTENSIVE VIEWS ACROSS THE NEARBY PLAINS. EASY WALKING, BUT CAN BE VERY MUDDY IN PLACES.

7

SAWLEY

has strong links with Fountains Abbey. Marmaduke Huby, the most famous of all Fountains' abbots, built Sawley church at the end of the 15th C. The church was rebuilt in 1769 and again a century later. The Sawley Arms is a popular hostelry noted for fine food.

★

Huby's Tower at Fountains Abbey is visible on the descent to Sawley from point 12, directly beyond the village. The White Horse of Kilburn can also be seen (20 miles).

the porch Sawley Church

Lacon Cross

LACON

was the name of a Royalist family who came from Shropshire to settle here in the early 17th C. Long before that, in medieval times, LACON HALL was a timber-framed house, and retains some of its original interior woodwork. It was rebuilt in stone c1550. LACON CROSS is of monastic origin — a wayside cross on a route used by the monks of Fountains Abbey.

Lacon Hall

BUTTERTON BRIDGE

has no parapet, and is so overgrown with turf, bracken and bluebells that it can be crossed almost unnoticed. To fully appreciate the bridge's height and obvious antiquity, go down the bank on its downstream side. It was built by the monks of Fountains.

–•–●–•–

EAVESTONE LAKE is seen at its best in May/June, when the rhododendrons are in bloom. The artificial lake was originally a monastic fishpond.

HOLLIN HILL FARM bristles with threatening and intimidatory signs — 'DANGER – KEEP OUT', 'NOT A PUBLIC RIGHT-OF-WAY', 'KEEP DOGS ON A LEAD', 'TRESPASSERS WILL BE PROSECUTED', 'OUR DOGS BITE' ETC. There also appears to be a bull in every field.

★

Should you manage to survive all of this, you will then have to cope with the nightmare of the farmyard at **GOWBUSK** – ferocious-looking dogs, junk everywhere and, in wet weather, a sea of liquid heaven-knows-what.

Eavestone Lake

MAP O.S. Explorer 26 Nidderdale

25

The walk is described as starting from Stack Point, a scenic woodland car park on the E shore of Swinsty Reservoir (Grid ref : 198 537) but there are two alternatives : –
Swinsty Moor car park, at the S end of Fewston Dam (Point 3 on the map – 186 538).
A59 at Blubberhouses, just below the church (Point 7 – 169 554).

Blubberhouses
A59
MUD!
ladder-stile
seat
Fewston Reservoir
x tree
fence
ruins
Thackray Beck
FB
On the author's last visit (Mar 04) the path from point 5 down to Thackray Beck was partially blocked by fallen trees.
Beecroft Moor Plantation
wire fence
barn
Fewston
Swinsty Lagoon – a haunt of anglers and herons
dam
car park, toilets, picnic area
Swinsty Moor Plantation
Swinsty Hall
Stack Point
Swinsty Reservoir
pump house
Swinsty Cottage
R. Washburn

ROUTE DIRECTIONS

① From car park follow road over causeway, take gate on R and forward along path into trees. Walk along top of dam and go R with track. ② Just past Swinsty Hall turn L (permissive FP) up track and continue along constructed path through plantation. ③ From car park go along road signposted Timble, Otley. ④ Just past first house on R turn R through gate (FP sign) to walled track opening out into small field. Take gate at its far corner, go L alongside wall and straight on along broad track into plantation. ⑤ Just past broken wall on R turn R (wm) down thin path. Cross footbridge and straight on, passing L of ruins and up enclosed track. Through gate and forward with fence on R. ⑥ When fence turns R go with it for a few yards, then bear slightly L away from it. Head for solitary tree (reservoir visible directly beyond it) then on to gate/stile (wm). Go straight on, following waymarked route through several fields. Eventually bear L through broken wall to a ladder-stile. Descend by wall on R. ⑦ Go L to car park, up steps and R along main road. On crossing bridge take path on R (FP sign). It runs full length of reservoir and finally descends flight of steps to road. ⑧ If you wish to include Fewston Church in the walk turn L along road. Keep R at junction (Norwood 1½) and follow road to Stack Point. For lakeside finish turn R towards dam and take downhill path on L.

NOTE : By using the road across Fewston dam the route could be adapted into two short, separate walks – Swinsty Circular (3 miles) and Fewston Circular (3½ miles – from Swinsty Moor or Blubberhouses).

THE WASHBURN VALLEY IS YORKSHIRE'S VERSION OF THE LAKE DISTRICT, AND ITS LAKES, THOUGH ARTIFICIAL, CAN RIVAL SOME OF THE NATURAL MERES OF CUMBRIA IN THE BEAUTY OF THEIR SETTINGS. THIS EASY AND GLORIOUS WALK ENCIRCLES THE TWO MIDDLE RESERVOIRS, TAKING FULL ADVANTAGE OF YORKSHIRE WATER'S EXCELLENT PERMISSIVE PATHS. THE PLEASANT FIELD ROUTE VIA THACKRAY BECK IS INCLUDED TO LEND VARIETY TO THE WALK, BUT IT CAN BE MUDDY. YOU CAN AVOID THIS SECTION BY USING (FROM POINT 3) A PERMISSIVE PATH ALONG THE W SHORE OF FEWSTON RESERVOIR.

8

The area's close proximity to the massive Leeds/Bradford conurbation ensures its tremendous popularity with ramblers, anglers, bird watchers and picnickers. On summer weekends you may need to arrive early to be sure of finding parking space.

Stack Point

THE CONIFER PLANTATIONS FORM A VALUABLE WILDLIFE HABITAT PROVIDING FOOD AND COVER FOR BIRDS SUCH AS SISKIN, COAL TIT, GOLDCREST, JAY, REDPOLL AND WOODPECKER. GREY SQUIRRELS ARE MUCH IN EVIDENCE. ON AND AROUND THE WATER YOU ARE LIKELY TO SEE GREAT CRESTED GREBE, HERON, TUFTED DUCK, GREY WAGTAIL AND GOOSANDER.

THE WASHBURN RESERVOIRS

THRUSCROSS
Completed 1967
Area 142 acres

A59

FEWSTON
Completed 1879
Area 156 acres

SWINSTY
Completed
1876. Area
156
acres

LINDLEY WOOD
Completed 1875
Area 117 acres

FEWSTON CHURCH

retains its 14th C. tower, but the rest of the church was rebuilt after being badly damaged by fire in 1697. The line of the steeply-pitched, and probably thatched, roof can be seen on the E wall of the tower. The massive wooden door in the porch was probably in use in 1697. The S wall of the chancel has a false door, visible only from outside the building. On sunny afternoons the rich stained glass in the chancel casts beautiful reflections across the altar. There are some interesting tombstones, including one which records burials on the 29th (in a non – leap year) and 30th Febuary (sic). E of the church is a massive box tomb bearing, in crude lettering, the inscription

SWINSTY HALL is a splendid Tudor and Jacobean house. It was built in the late 16th C.

John Brerey's tomb

IHon BRERY dieΛ 1613

MAP O.S. Explorer 27 Lower Wharfedale and the Washburn Valley.

27

9 FROSTROW FELLS

7 MILES

P Barth Bridge, on the Dent-Sedbergh road about a mile NW of Dent. Parking space on either side of road on W side of bridge.
Grid ref: 694 879

High Hollins
Side Farm
⑤
High Side
⑥
Clatter Beck
⑦ wall
thin path
pond
g/s
walled enclosures
clear path boggy in places
★
Holebeck Gill
FROSTROW FELLS
superb green track
FP
Gap Wood
★
Gap
Hewthwaite
⑧
⑨
⑩
Burton Hill
⑪
Leakses
Helms Knott
△ 975'
wall
bog
④
g/s
Long Moor
FP
pond
⑫
Mire House
1635
cut
g
g
bog
Lunds
③
barn
R. Dee
FB
DENTDALE
★
monument
②
①
BARTH BRIDGE

ROUTE DIRECTIONS

① Go along main road away from bridge. In 100 yds turn R along lane. ② Go L at fork. In 60 yds turn R (FP Hining Hill 1¼). Go up green path to stile. Climb field to stile well to L of buildings. Forward through two more stiles and up farm road. ③ At farm turn L (FP Sedbergh 3), then R at barn to climb walled green track. When it ends, continue alongside wall on L to gate/stile in crosswall. ④ Turn L to follow wall. When wall bends L keep straight ahead (clear path) to descend to gill on R. Before reaching wall path swings L. Cross gate/ladder-stile into stony lane leading to tarmac lane. ⑤ Take stile on L (FP High Side) and up field to stile (wm) at RH corner. Through gate and follow farm road. Pass R of farm to stile (wm) and up field to gate. ⑥ Turn R to follow wall. When wall turns R keep straight on along thin, level path across moor. Pass R of some small, walled enclosures. ⑦ Turn L along cart-track. Take L fork up to gate/stile. Follow wall on L. Pass through wood to farm beyond (Gap). ⑧ Pass R of farm and take stile on L (FP sign). Head for next farm (Hewthwaite). ⑨ Pass R of farm. Cross farm road to stile and follow waymarks to next farm (Burton Hill). ⑩ Through farmyard to ladder-stile on L (FP sign). Head for next farm (Leakses). ⑪ Follow waymarks to pass in front of house and down to fence-stile. Drop diagonally L to stile, then turn R down to road. Go L along road. ⑫ At Mire House turn R (FP Monument 1¼), through gate and down track. Cross watercut and bear slightly L to stile. At river go L along embankment. Turn R along road.

28

THE FROSTROW FELLS ARE LOW, GRASSY MOORS SEPARATING THE LOWER REACHES OF DENTDALE AND GARSDALE. THIS FINE WALK OFFERS INTIMATE VIEWS OF THE TWO PLEASANTLY WOODED DALES WITH THEIR RICH HAY MEADOWS SET AGAINST CONTRASTING BACKCLOTHS OF DRAMATIC MOUNTAIN SCENERY. THE ROUTE, THOUGH UNDULATING, HAS NO STEEP GRADIENTS. IT IS NOT RECOMMENDED IN MIST, AND IN WET WEATHER CAN BE EXTREMELY MUDDY, WITH ONE PARTICULARLY VILE SWAMP IN THE LANE ABOVE LUNDS.

9

DENTDALE

This small, secluded and supremely beautiful valley is a sort of 'border territory' between the Yorkshire Dales and the Lake District, though its unique atmosphere is not quite that of either the Dales or the Lakes. Dentdale was originally settled by Irish-Norse colonisers – sheep farmers of the 9th and 10th centuries. A feature of the landscape is the remarkable number of farmhouses – most of them whitewashed. We shall pass a string of these ancient farmsteads – Gap, Hewthwaite, Burton Hill and Leakses – between points 8 and 11.

In the 17th C. **LUNDS** was known as 'The slatehouse' for its roof of slates or flags was a most uncommon feature; most small farm-houses in those days were thatched with heather (ling-thatched).

FROM POINT 4 ONWARDS THE VIEW IS DOMINATED BY THE HOWGILL FELLS, RISING LOFTILY BEHIND SEDBERGH. AT A FIELD GATE NEAR THE LITTLE STREAM JUST BEFORE SIDE FARM PAUSE AWHILE TO GAZE ACROSS TO THE RIGHT OF THE HOWGILLS UPON A SCENE OF EXQUISITE PASTORAL CHARM.

High Side as it looked in 1990, before renovation.

This big boulder, just beyond point 7, makes an excellent natural seat.

The **RIVERSIDE PATH** at the end of the walk is easy and pleasant. Here, where the River Dee now meanders and sometimes floods, was once a glacial lake. It is a good area for bird-watching, attracting many interesting species of waders and ducks. It is known that in medieval times there was a mill near **BARTH BRIDGE**, but all traces of the building have long since disappeared.

Burton Hill Farm

MAPS O.S. Explorer OL2 Yorkshire Dales Southern and Western areas AND O.S. Explorer OL19 Howgill Fells.

10 HARDRAW FORCE

7 MILES

P Hawes. Large car park (pay and display) at National Park Centre, off the A684 Bainbridge road.
Grid ref: 875 899

ROUTE DIRECTIONS

① From corner of car park near toilets go up path and R along road. Take gate on L to flagged path through field. Rejoin road and follow it over bridge. ② Take stile on R (SP Sedbusk 1¼). Forward over footbridge and up to stile. Climb field to stile at RH corner. ③ Cross lane to stile. Take stepped path and climb to pass L of a barn to stile. Go R along lane. ④ At junction turn L to go straight through village and up rough lane (concrete initially). ⑤ Take ladder-stile/gate on L to sunken green path. Clear path climbs to swing L above small copse, through two gates, then up to L of low scar. At a marker-post path bears L to climb to a bridleway guidepost. ⑥ Go L up stony vehicle track, which soon swings R to become a broad, green, level, rutted track. ⑦ Ignore vehicle track descending L. Keep straight on (BW sign) along green path. ⑧ Just after crossing a depression fork L up thinner path. When it peters out keep straight on to a pair of cairns (viewpoint). Turn sharp R to follow level path with marker-posts. Cross rocky stream (may be dry) then descend cart-track (wm) to road. ⑨ Go L down road. ⑩ At cottages turn R down lane (Shaw Ghyll Caravan Site). At bottom of hill turn sharp L through gate (FP Shaw Gill) and follow flagged path downstream to gate, then up walled lane to road. Turn R. ⑪ Turn R (FP Hardraw) along farm road. Take stile on R of farm and descend flagged path to village. ⑫ Access to Hardraw Force is through Green Dragon Inn. On return take path opposite inn (PW sign). Fork L along flagged path. When flags end keep

⑨ Shivery Gill
△ shapely cairn
Pike Hill MP x ⑧
★
Sowry Head
Fred's x c High Quarry
Bench x ⑦
x BW sign
Abbotside Common
North Rakes Hill
broad, level, rutted track x GP
Low Clint
plateau High Clint ⑥
Fossdale Reservoir (covered)
x MP
x kiln
kennels
FOSSDALE
⑩ High Shaw
High Pasture Gate
easy bit
copse
wall
Shaw Gill Wood ★
HARDRAW FORCE ⑪
★
hotel West House
SEDBUSK
lane ④
Stone House barn lane
Shutt Lane ⑤
gls
⑫ HARDRAW
flagged path
gls gls
wall ③
gls
Kingfishers can sometimes be seen in the vicinity of Haylands Bridge.
Haylands Bridge
mast x
cricket ground
flagged path ②
R. Ure
FB
①
HAWES — National Park Centre Car Park, Toilets

cont. on next page

AN UPPER WENSLEYDALE WALK OF GREAT VARIETY AND CHARM, WITH SWEEPING VIEWS OF THE DALE FROM THE FINE HIGH-LEVEL TRAVERSE ABOVE SEDBUSK. THE IDEAL TIME TO DO THE WALK IS LATE SPRING, WHEN THE WOODS AT HARDRAW ARE AT THEIR LOVELIEST, AND PREFERABLY AFTER A SPELL OF WET WEATHER HAS ENHANCED THE DISPLAY OF ENGLAND'S HIGHEST WATERFALL. THE FIRST PART OF THE WALK IS STRENUOUS, WITH A CLIMB OF 1,000' FROM HAYLANDS BRIDGE TO POINT 6.

IN MIST THE SECTION BETWEEN POINTS 7 AND 9 COULD BE AWKWARD

ROUTE DIRECTIONS cont: straight on to come alongside wall on R. Turn R to follow road back to Hawes.

HAWES

Haylands Bridge

is unlike most Dales market towns in being situated near the head of the dale, and at 850' is the highest market town in Yorkshire. Most of its buildings are Victorian, with here and there a few survivors from the 17th and 18th C. The AUCTION MART is one of the most important livestock markets in the Dales. The PARISH CHURCH OF ST. MARGARET was built in 1850 to replace a chapel-of-ease which had existed since c 1480. The WENSLEYDALE CREAMERY (which has a popular Visitor Centre) makes the only true Wensleydale cheese in the world. Hawes has a very good range of shops, hotels and guest houses.

———— •–●–• ————

HARDRAW CHURCH, DEDICATED TO ST. MARY AND ST. JOHN, WAS ORIGINALLY BUILT IN THE LATE 16TH C. AS A CHAPEL-OF-EASE. IN 1763 THE BUILDING WAS DESCRIBED AS 'RUINOUS', AND THE PRESENT CHURCH WAS BUILT IN 1879. THE REV. ROBERT PINCK WAS VICAR HERE FROM 1854 TO 1913 – AN INCREDIBLE 59 YEARS. HE IS COMMEMORATED BY THE EAST WINDOW.

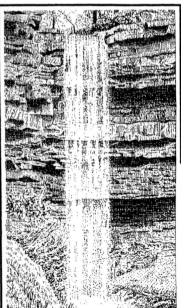

HARDRAW FORCE plunges in a single leap of 96' at the head of a wooded gorge. The land is privately owned, and the only access is through the Green Dragon Inn, where a charge is made. The gorge has remarkable acoustics, and an annual brass band contest is held here (note the circular walled bandstand). The rock wall behind the waterfall reveals strata of the 'Yordedale cycle'! At the top is hard black limestone, forming a considerable overhang. At the foot are beds of shale, and the middle section consists of layers of sandstone. The French stuntman Charles Blondin once walked over the waterfall on a tightrope, pausing midway to cook an omelette.

Hardraw Force

MAP | O.S. Explorer OL 30 Yorkshire Dales Northern and Central areas.

Gunnerside. Parking area at centre of village, on west side of bridge. Grid ref: 951 982

ROUTE DIRECTIONS

① Cross bridge and turn L along riverside path. Just before house turn R (FP sign) up steps. Through gate and turn L to follow clear path up-valley. ② Follow signpost Gunnerside Gill Woodland Path. ③ At end of woodland cross footbridge and two wall-stiles. Forward with wall on L through two more stiles to pass L of crushing mill ruins. ④ Just beyond ruins take stile (wm) in wire fence to a rising path. Cross another stile to reach slit-stile in wall. Continue up clear path. ⑤ Pass ruins and keep to main (rising) path. At guidepost stay on rising path (SP Blakethwaite Dams). ⑥ A path zig-zags steeply down L to ruins of smelt mill. USE THIS PATH IN WET WEATHER, WHEN THE STREAM WILL BE DIFFICULT TO FORD AT POINT 7. Otherwise remain on green path. ⑦ Ford stream above waterfall and return downstream on a clear path. ⑧ Just before kiln fork L to drop steeply to ruins. Ford the small tributary stream to broad green path up hillside. Keep R at a fork. ⑨ At track junction go L across gill to gate/stile and vehicle track. ⑩ When track begins to swing R turn L (small cairn) and descend directly towards houses of Gunnerside. At fence go R down sunken path, then bear L down to stile into village.

Blind Gill

kiln x

ruin

green path

Blakethwaite Smelt Mill

⑧ ⑦ ⑥

Gorton Hush

scree

Friarfold Hush

North Hush

Bunton Hush

GP x

green path

⑤ old crushing mill (Bunton Mine)

Melbecks Moor

⑨

Botcher Gill

9/S

level path

wall

Silver Hill

air tank x

excellent green path

Sir Francis Mine

④ old crushing mill (Sir Francis Mine)

vehicle track

③ FB

old mine road

Jingle Pot Edge

②

⑩

fence

The old mine road gives fine views down Gunnerside Gill and across Swaledale to Whitaside Moor, but in itself is rather tedious. The monotony may be alleviated by looking across the valley to pick out features of the outward route.

① GUNNERSIDE

King's Head
toilets (immaculate)

Little Bridge and King's Head, Gunnerside

LEAD MINING AND SMELTING, ONCE AN IMPORTANT INDUSTRY IN THE DALES, WENT INTO SUDDEN DECLINE TOWARDS THE END OF THE 19th CENTURY. THIS WALK PROVIDES A FASCINATING EXPLORATION OF SOME OF THE ABANDONED MINE WORKINGS WHICH ABOUND ON THE NORTH SIDE OF SWALEDALE. THE WALK PASSES FROM SYLVAN WOODLAND, WHERE BLUEBELLS MAKE A FINE SHOW IN MAY, TO WILD, STARK DESOLATION. CLEAR PATHS THROUGHOUT, BUT ROUGH UNDERFOOT IN PLACES.

11

☠ ON NO ACCOUNT SHOULD YOU ENTER ANY OF THE OLD MINE LEVELS. THEY ARE DECAYING, UNSTABLE, VERY OFTEN FLOODED AND HIGHLY DANGEROUS.

GUNNERSIDE

The village was once two individual settlements separated by the beck. The name Gunnerside applied to the village on the west side of the stream; that on the east was known as Lodge Green. Between the late-18th and early-19th centuries Gunnerside grew to become one of the most important lead-mining centres in the Dales. In the wake of the industry's demise, many people left to find employment in the mills of Lancashire and the West Riding, or to emigrate to America. The bridge was built in 1832 to replace a wooden one.

GUNNERSIDE GILL

is one of the longest, narrowest and most dramatic of Swaledale's many tributary valleys. The trees in the lower valley are typical of the species which would have covered most of the area for hundreds of years.

SIR FRANCIS MINE

THIS MINE WAS STARTED IN 1864, AND ITS OWNER, SIR GEORGE DENIS, NAMED IT AFTER HIS SON. THE RUINS AT POINT 4 ARE THE REMAINS OF A DRESSING FLOOR ON WHICH THE MINERAL ORE WAS CRUSHED AND GALENA (LEAD ORE) SEPARATED. THE ROW OF BAYS WERE FOR THE STORAGE OF ORE. FROM HERE THE GALENA WAS TAKEN BY PACK PONY OVER THE HILL FOR SMELTING AT SURRENDER MILL (SEE WALK 16). ACROSS THE BECK IS A RUINED BUILDING WHICH WAS THE MINE'S OFFICE AND STABLES, AND A RUSTY OLD COMPRESSED AIR TANK JUST ABOVE IT WAS ONCE USED TO POWER THE ROCK DRILLS. THE MINE CLOSED IN 1882.

Sir Francis Mine - ruins of office and stables.

BUNTON MINE

The ruins at point 5 were the offices, stables, smithy, gunpowder store etc. of the Bunton Mine. The waterwheel pit is just below the track, as is a row of bunkers for ore.

old level, Bunton Mine

Until the end of the 18th C. '**HUSHING**' was a common method of obtaining lead. Where a vein was suspected on the hillside, a stream would be dammed on the moor above. The dam would then be smashed, releasing a torrent of water to tear away the soil and so expose the vein. This was repeated many times, gouging out a ravine or 'hush'.

BLAKETHWAITE SMELT MILL

Built c 1820. Amongst the ruins can be seen 4 iron pillars which supported the arches in front of twin furnaces. Behind the furnaces was the waterwheel driving the bellows, and behind the wheel was a roasting hearth. The building with 4 big arches was a peat store.

MAP O.S. Explorer OL 30 Yorkshire Dales Northern and Central areas.

ROUTE DIRECTIONS

Malham. Large car park (pay and display) at National Park Centre. Grid ref: 900 626

① Walk towards village. At first building on R (smithy) cross bridge and turn R to follow gravel path to Janet's Foss. ② Turn R along lane. Pass Gordale Bridge and when lane bends R take gate on L and gravel path to Gordale Scar. ③ Retrace steps. Cross Gordale Bridge to gate (SP Malham Cove). Follow gravel path and climb with wall on R to gate. Up next field to steps/gate then follow gravel path. ④ Cross lane to ladder-stile (FP Malham Cove 1¼). Follow cart-track, which soon becomes a broad, green path. ⑤ At guidepost by wall-corner turn R along green path. Follow it up a small valley and on across the moor. Ignore any paths branching L. ⑥ Just beyond some ponds fork R (FP Malham Tarn 1). Cross ladder-stile and take LH path. ⑦ Cross road and go straight on (PW sign) to tarn. Return to road and go R. Turn L through gate (PW sign). Forward to guidepost then head L (FP Malham Cove, Water Sinks).

Follow clear path along RH side of wall and through Comb Scar. ⑧ Turn sharp L over stile (FP Malham Cove, Malham Village) to descend dry valley. Cross top of Cove (see NOTE below) to gate at far end of limestone pavement. Down steps and fork R along gravel path. ⑨ Cross clapper bridge and climb diagonally R. At top of rise keep straight on along obvious field path, which eventually becomes a walled track leading down to village.

Map labels: Malham Tarn, PW, Malham Water, GP, Water Sinks, wall, ponds, cave, Comb Scar, Prior Rakes, boulders, Watlowes (dry valley), Trougate, wall, The Cove, steps, clapper bridge ruin, lane, Grey Gill, Gordale Scar, Malham Beck, ancient boundaries, Cawden (reef knoll), lane, Gordale Bridge, Janet's Foss, Little Gordale, barn, MALHAM, Nat. Park Centre car park, toilets, barn, concrete bridge, Gordale Beck, barn

NOTE: You are strongly advised to cross the top of The Cove via the raised grassy outcrops to the R of the limestone pavement. Small children and dogs should **ALWAYS** be taken this way. Crossing the pavement demands **CARE** and **CONCENTRATION**, especially in wet weather, and a fall into one of the deep grikes could cause serious injury.

THE NATIONAL TRUST
BOMBEY'S BARN
MALHAM TARN ESTATE

BOMBEY'S BARN, now a ruin, is passed just beyond point 9.

👣 MALHAM IS ONE OF THE MOST FAMOUS WALKING AREAS IN BRITAIN, AND ITS FAME IS RICHLY DESERVED. THE LIMESTONE SCENERY IS EVERYWHERE SUPERB, AND AT GORDALE SCAR AND THE COVE IS ABSOLUTELY SENSATIONAL. OTHER HIGHLIGHTS ALONG THE WAY ARE A PRETTY WATERFALL, A LARGE AND BEAUTIFUL TARN, AN IMPRESSIVE DRY VALLEY AND A MAGNIFICENT LIMESTONE PAVEMENT. GENERALLY EASY WALKING, BUT VERY ROUGH UNDERFOOT IN THE VICINITY OF COMB SCAR. AVOID MALHAM AT WEEKENDS, UNLESS YOU DON'T MIND QUEUEING AT STILES.

12

FOR A SHORTER WALK (4¼ MILES), OMITTING THE TARN AND THE DRY VALLEY, DESCEND FROM POINT 5 DIRECTLY TO THE TOP OF THE COVE.

MALHAM

has a resident population of only about 130, but its unique attractions mean that it is always thronged with visitors. The village has many ancient and interesting buildings, and its rustic charm is undeniable. An excellent leaflet - 'Malham village walk', obtainable from the National Park Centre, provides a circular walk of less than one hour describing the historical features of this utterly fascinating place.

JANET'S FOSS is a pretty waterfall set in the lovely little dell of Gordale Beck. There's an information board here.

Monk Bridge was built in 1636 and has since been widened.

★GORDALE SCAR, ONE OF THE MOST SPECTACULAR LAND-FORMS IN ENGLAND, IS AN AWE-INSPIRING GORGE WITH SHEER WALLS TOWERING TO A HEIGHT OF 150 FEET

THE TARN has an area of 153 acres, but is nowhere more than 14' deep. In the midst of limestone, which will not hold surface water, the tarn lies on a bed of slate. The outflow stream, MALHAM WATER, manages to travel for only about half a mile before seeping underground at WATER SINKS.

WATLOWES is a superb dry valley. The wall along its length dates from monastic times, when it divided the lands of Fountains Abbey in the W from those of Bolton Priory in the E.

THE COVE

is without any doubt Malham's N°1 attraction. This dramatic limestone cliff - 650' wide and nearly 300' high - is the finest piece of rock scenery in the country. The limestone pavement above it is fissured by cracks called 'grikes,' and many plants - some quite rare - thrive in their shady recesses. The stream issuing from the base of the cliff is NOT that which disappears at Water Sinks.

MAP O.S. Explorer OL2 Yorkshire Dales Southern and Western areas.

13 PENYGHENT GILL

6¼ MILES

P Litton. About ⅓ mile W of the village a rough lane leads down between walls to a stone bridge spanning the R.Skirfare. There is limited parking space on the lane's grass verges. DON'T BLOCK ANY FIELD GATES.

Grid ref: 898 742

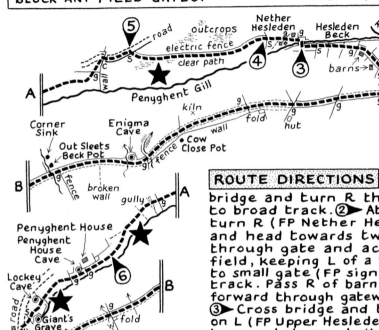

ROUTE DIRECTIONS

① Cross bridge and turn R through gate to broad track. ② At guidepost turn R (FP Nether Hesleden ¾) and head towards two barns. Go through gate and across next field, keeping L of a wall-corner to small gate (FP sign) into walled track. Pass R of barn and continue forward through gateways and stiles. ③ Cross bridge and take gate on L (FP Upper Hesleden). Forward to pass between buildings to gate. Keep straight on up green path (FP Upper Hesleden) to ladder-stile. ④ Climb alongside fence on R to road. ⑤ Go L along road. Immediately after crossing cattle-grid turn L (FP Silverdale Rd 1¼) down path. Go through gate in crosswall and follow clear path as it swings R and heads up-valley. ⑥ Pass well below farm (Penyghent House), keeping L of a wall-corner. From second gate bear slightly R (FP sign) uphill to guidepost, then resume a level course. Cross rocky stream (Lockey Gill) and bear L down to fence to view Giant's Grave Caves. Follow fence forward, through stile and go L up tarmac road. ⑦ Turn sharp L (SP Bridle Road to Litton) along wide track. No further directions are necessary — just follow this track all the way back to New Bridge.

LITTONDALE is a U-shaped glacial valley dominated by long limestone scars. In Norman times it was a hunting forest belonging to the Percy family of Northumberland. On being acquired by Fountains Abbey the dale became a sheep-rearing estate. Charles Kingsley called the valley 'Vendale' and Wordsworth (right) named it 'Amerdale'. Littondale is noted for its beauty, its superb field barns and its wealth of birdlife.

AN EXHILARATING HIGH-LEVEL CIRCUIT OF ONE OF THE THREE SPECTACULAR RAVINES WHICH CUT THROUGH THE MOORS ALONG THE SOUTH-WEST SIDE OF LITTONDALE. SOME SPLENDID LIMESTONE SCENERY IS ENCOUNTERED AT THE HEAD OF THE RAVINE BEFORE RETURNING TO LITTONDALE BY WAY OF A DELIGHTFUL OLD PACKHORSE ROUTE ACROSS WILD, LONELY MOORS. THE VIEWS ARE QUITE SUPERB. THERE'S A LONG CLIMB FROM NETHER HESLEDEN TO THE ROAD AT POINT 5; THE REST IS VERY EASY.

The **RIVER SKIRFARE** is formed by the merging of Foxup Beck and Cosh Beck at Foxup Bridge, and flows for some 8½ miles to join the Wharfe at Amerdale Dub, just above Kilnsey. During dry spells the Skirfare tends to disappear underground in places— a fact which has probably saved Littondale from becoming a reservoir.

— Nether Hesleden

★

Littondale is one of the very few dales unscarred by the ravages of lead-mining.

POTHOLES AND CAVES

abound in the vicinity of Penyghent Gill. Only those close to, and easily accessible from, the route are shown on the map, and the fun lies rather in locating than exploring them. **PENYGHENT HOUSE CAVE** is in a hollow on the right, just past Penyghent House Farm. The large entrance leads straight into an impressive streamway, which can be explored with the aid of a good torch — but you won't go far before getting wet feet. The entrance to **LOCKEY CAVE** is on the true right bank of Lockey Gill some 20 yards below the road bridge. It may be entered and penetrated for some distance, but is low, narrow, uncomfortable and filthy. **GIANT'S GRAVE CAVES**, from which emerge the waters of Penyghent Gill, are in a bouldery depression below a fence on the

Penyghent House Cave

left just beyond Lockey Gill. **RIFT CAVE** lies 30 yards to the right of the track in a shallow valley. The entrance to **OUT SLEETS BECK POT**, an extensive system, is in the true right bank of a small stream, about 60 yards below the track and not too easy to find. There is access via a gate by the track, but it is not a right-of-way. **CORNER SINK** is a further 60 yards downstream. **ENIGMA CAVE** is by a small stream between the track and the wall. **COW CLOSE POT**, which descends to a depth of 115 feet (though not in one pitch) lies in a small patch of clints about 30 yards from the wall on the right of the track.

Lapwing

These moors support a rich variety of bird-life. Curlew and lapwing are particularly prevalent.

MAP OS Explorer OL 30 Yorkshire Dales Northern and Central areas.

6½ MILES

P Wharfe. The road from Austwick to Helwith Bridge bends sharply as it passes close to the hamlet. Just below the bend, by a barn, there is space to park a couple of cars, and there is the odd space here and there along the roadside verges.

Grid ref (barn):784 694
DON'T BLOCK ANY GATES.

ROUTE DIRECTIONS

① Walk up road to bend and turn L down track (Private road. Public footpath and bridleway only.) At fork go R (BW sign). ② Pass two barns close together, and in 200yds take wall-stile on R. Go straight along field to gateway, then climb shallow, bouldery depression. ③ At top of rise keep L to gate/stile. Go straight ahead along two fields to stile at far LH corner. Follow green lane to its end at a gate, and continue up green path. ④ Pass between some small outcrops then turn L to take RH of three paths. It soon swings R to head towards Penyghent. ⑤ Cross ladder-stile and go L (SP Horton in R 1¾) alongside wall. From next stile go ½ R (SP Horton in Ribblesdale). At guidepost turn L (SP Ingleborough) up track to double ladder-stile. Continue along clear path. ⑥ At guidepost turn L (BW Clapham 3¾). Cross gate/ladder-stile and immediately take small gate on L. Drop steeply into hollow and go forward along green path. ⑦ Just beyond its lowest point the path forks. Go R to follow clear path through limestone pavements to ladder-stile. ⑧ Descend to head away along green path, soon joining another coming in from R. Pass R of farm and through two waymarked gates to join farm road. ⑨ Turn L (BW Wharfe 1¼) along walled lane. After passing the two barns at point 2 fork L along the narrow upper path to return to Wharfe and the starting point.

(map labels)
GP × Sulber Gate
clear path
clear level path
double ladder-stile
⑥
Sulber Nick
gls
GP
Thieves' Moss
⑦
FPsign
wall
⑤
good path
outcrops
wall
Beggar's Stile
Moughton Scars
⑧
ruin
⑤
green path
Austwick Beck Head
Capple Bank
spring
④
gls
wall
Moughton
Crummack Farm
splendid green lane
farm road
fold
White Stone Lane
c
⑨
Studrigg Scar
gls
slab bridge
③
barn
White Stone Wood
Austwick Beck
②
barns
WHARFE
barn P
①

JUNIPER is not a common shrub in N. England, but thrives on Moughton's limestone pavements. The juice of the berries is used to flavour gin, and 'oil of juniper', obtainable from chemists, is an effective remedy for flatulence!

THIS FASCINATING RAMBLE TAKES THE WALKER FROM THE LEAFY LANES OF WHARFE TO THE GREAT LIMESTONE PLATEAUX WHICH ENCIRCLE THE LONELY VALLEY OF CRUMMACK. THE SCENERY OF THESE UPLANDS IS QUITE UNFORGETTABLE – A WEIRD, WONDERFUL AND MAGICAL WORLD OF LONG, CURVING LIMESTONE CLIFFS SWEEPING AROUND HUGE AMPHITHEATRES OF GLEAMING CLINTS. EXCELLENT TRACKS AND PATHS THROUGHOUT.

CRUMMACK DALE

Cottage at Wharfe

is one of the most delectable and captivating of Yorkshire's small dales. The limestone scenery at the head of the valley is spellbinding, and will have geologists in raptures. This is exactly how the land must have looked after the last Ice Age.

← vultures
HORTON 1¼

★

As you saunter along **SULBER NICK** you may meet dishevelled and weary-looking walkers, some perhaps reduced to crawling on hands and knees. They will be completing the last mile or so of the 24 mile 3 Peaks marathon. Spare a word of encouragement (or sympathy) as they stagger by.

WHARFE is a tiny, tree-shaded, secluded hamlet hidden away down flowery bridleways.

AUSTWICK BECK HEAD

ON THE SOUTH-EASTERN SLOPES OF SIMON FELL IS AN AREA KNOWN AS 'THE ALLOTMENT', WHERE THE SURFACE STREAMS, ON REACHING THE LIMESTONE, SINK INTO A MULTITUDE OF RIFTS AND POTHOLES. THE STREAMS CONTINUE THEIR JOURNEY UNDERGROUND UNTIL THEY REACH THE BASE OF THE GREAT SCAR LIMESTONE, WHERE THE UNDERLYING IMPERMEABLE ROCK FORCES THEM TO THE SURFACE, THE COMBINED WATERS EMERGING – IMPRESSIVELY AFTER RAIN – FROM TWO LOW CAVES AT AUSTWICK BECK HEAD.

INGLEBOROUGH 2½   FP HORTON IN R 1½

PLEASE KEEP DOGS ON A LEAD

Beggar's Stile

Moughton is pronounced 'Moot'n.

Guidepost at point 6.

Crummack Farm

MAP   O.S. Explorer OL2 Yorkshire Dales Southern and Western areas.

15 ILKLEY MOOR

6¼ MILES

P Ilkley. Large car park below Cow and Calf Rocks, by the Ilkley - Burley Woodhead road about 250yds on the Ilkley side of the Cow and Calf Hotel.

Grid ref : 132 467

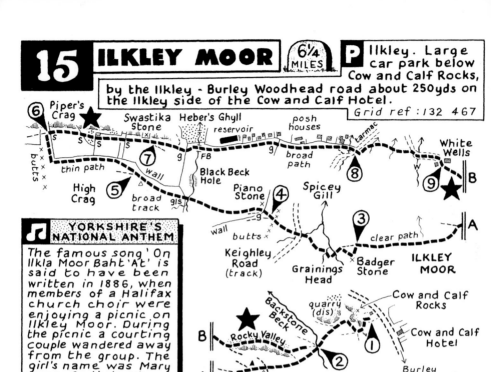

ROUTE DIRECTIONS

①▶ Climb flagged path towards rocks then turn L up another flagged path. At top follow path R. At big quarry path swings L and heads towards highest point on skyline. ②▶ Cross stream and take LH path heading for highest point. Pass big heap of stones and straight on up to summit cairn. Take middle of three paths, heading towards two distant masts. Follow clear path, ignoring any paths forking R. ③▶ Detour L to Badger Stone (seat beside it) then go R to rejoin original path. Cross an unsurfaced road and climb broad track. ④▶ At grouse butt fork R to small gate. Follow clear, level path. Cross stream to gate/stile and up broad path. ⑤▶ When wall on R disappears from view, path forks. Go R to come alongside wall. Don't cross it. When wall turns R go with it. ⑥▶ Take wall-stile(wm) on R. Follow clear path. ⑦▶ At Swastika Stone fork L (wm). At next fork keep R to swing-gate, then fork L down to wall-side path. ⑧▶ Cross road and go L (wm) down path. It soon swings R and heads for white building (White Wells). ⑨▶ Pass to R of main building and up broad path (SP Millenium (*sic*) Way). Just before reaching a steep, stepped section fork L (wm). Follow path up through Rocky Valley, then fork L (wm) to descend to stream at point 2. Retrace outward route to car park.

ILKLEY MOOR IS A PUBLIC COMMON, AND THERE ARE NO RESTRICTIONS ON THE USE OF ITS PROFUSION OF PATHS. THIS IS AN EXCELLENT WALK FOR DOGS.

A BRACING WALK ON GOOD PATHS ALONG THE EDGE OF WHAT IS PERHAPS THE MOST FAMOUS TRACT OF MOORLAND IN BRITAIN. THE ROUTE, BESIDES OFFERING PANORAMIC VIEWS OF LOWER WHARFEDALE, VISITS A SUCCESSION OF PLACES OF INTEREST, AND THE RUGGED GRITSTONE SCENERY IS QUITE MAGNIFICENT. THERE ARE TWO FAIRLY STRENUOUS SECTIONS - FROM THE STARTING POINT TO CRANSHAW THORN HILL (WHEN YOU'RE FRESH) AND A LONG CLIMB FROM BELOW WHITE WELLS TO THE TOP OF ROCKY VALLEY (WHEN YOU'RE NOT). A GOOD WALK FOR DOGS.

15

COW AND CALF ROCKS

a famous and popular attraction much-frequented by rock-climbers, bear no resemblance whatsoever to the animals whose names they carry.

Many of the rocks and boulders on these moors bear strange carvings of great antiquity. The most common are the 'CUP AND RING' markings - small hollows within a circle or concentric circles. The BADGER STONE has an elaborate design carved on its south face, although it is badly eroded and was damaged by battle practice during the second world war.

The 'Piano Stone'

The famous SWASTIKA STONE, protected from vandalism by iron railings, displays a rounded version of the ancient Indo-European good-luck symbol, which is also incorporated in the design on the Badger Stone. It is believed to date from c 2,000 BC. The original is the less obvious carving on the main rock. The one at the front is a replica for ease of viewing.

The carved pattern on the Swastika Stone.

WHITE WELLS

was built in the 1760s as a bath house for Ilkley folk, who could there enjoy a dip in the cold but pure and supposedly curative waters of the moorland spring. The growing popularity of hydropathy in the early 19th C. turned Ilkley into a fashionable spa town, and many of its hotels and large houses date from this period. Patients were transported up the moor by donkey. The sturdy building, which still contains the original well, is now a cafe and visitor centre.

MAP   O.S. Explorer 27 Lower Wharfedale / Washburn Valley.

16 HARD LEVEL GILL

5½ MILES

P Surrender Bridge, which is on the moorland road running north from Feetham near a junction with another minor road coming up from Healaugh. Plenty of parking space at the road junction.

Grid ref : 989 998

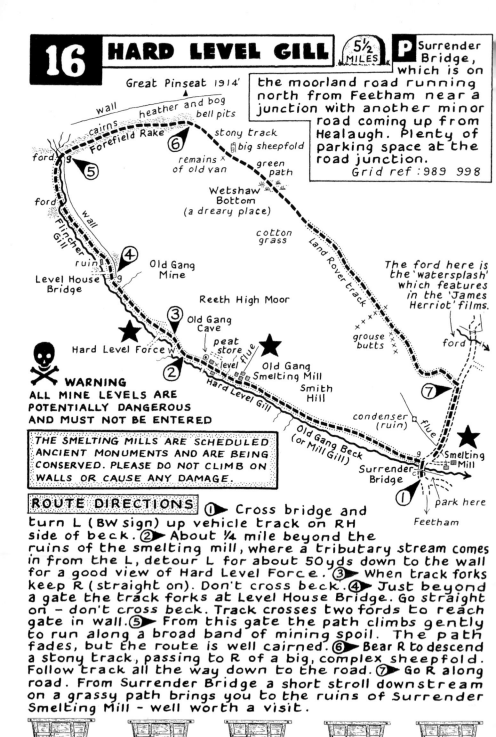

Great Pinseat 1914'

wall

heather and bog

bell pits

cairns

Forefield Rake

stony track

big sheepfold

ford g

⑤

⑥

remains of old van

green path

ford

Flincher Gill

wall

Wetshaw Bottom (a dreary place)

cotton grass

Land Rover track

ruin

④

Old Gang Mine

Level House Bridge g

Reeth High Moor

The ford here is the 'watersplash' which features in the 'James Herriot' films.

③

Old Gang Cave

peat store

grouse butts

ford

Hard Level Force

level flue

Old Gang Smelting Mill

②

Smith Hill

Hard Level Gill

☠ **WARNING**
ALL MINE LEVELS ARE POTENTIALLY DANGEROUS AND MUST NOT BE ENTERED

⑦

condenser (ruin) flue

Old Gang Beck (or Mill Gill)

Surrender Bridge

g

Smelting Mill

THE SMELTING MILLS ARE SCHEDULED ANCIENT MONUMENTS AND ARE BEING CONSERVED. PLEASE DO NOT CLIMB ON WALLS OR CAUSE ANY DAMAGE.

①

park here

Feetham

ROUTE DIRECTIONS

① Cross bridge and turn L (BW sign) up vehicle track on RH side of beck. ② About ¼ mile beyond the ruins of the smelting mill, where a tributary stream comes in from the L, detour L for about 50 yds down to the wall for a good view of Hard Level Force. ③ When track forks keep R (straight on). Don't cross beck. ④ Just beyond a gate the track forks at Level House Bridge. Go straight on – don't cross beck. Track crosses two fords to reach gate in wall. ⑤ From this gate the path climbs gently to run along a broad band of mining spoil. The path fades, but the route is well cairned. ⑥ Bear R to descend a stony track, passing to R of a big, complex sheepfold. Follow track all the way down to the road. ⑦ Go R along road. From Surrender Bridge a short stroll downstream on a grassy path brings you to the ruins of Surrender Smelting Mill - well worth a visit.

NOT A PRETTY WALK. THE 'SCENERY' THROUGHOUT CAN ONLY BE DESCRIBED AS STARK, GRIM AND DESOLATE. THIS SHOULD BE DECLARED AN AOUU (AREA OF OUTSTANDING UNNATURAL UGLINESS). IT IS, HOWEVER, A WALK WHICH **MUST** BE DONE (THOUGH PROBABLY ONLY ONCE) AND WHICH WILL APPEAL TO THOSE WALKERS WHOSE IMAGINATION IS STIRRED BY THE ATMOSPHERIC REMAINS OF A BYGONE INDUSTRY. ALTHOUGH A HEIGHT OF NEARLY 2000' IS REACHED, THE CLIMBING – ON OLD MINING TRACKS – IS VERY GENTLE, WITH NO STILES TO IMPEDE PROGRESS. A GOOD DOGGY-WALK.

16

OLD GANG SMELT MILL

The most striking feature of the extensive ruins is the well-preserved chimney. The building to which this belonged was used for roasting the lead ore (galena) prior to smelting. The actual smelting took place in the long building next to the path, which had 4 furnaces. A long flue carried the poisonous fumes up the hillside. Above the mill on the moor can be seen the stone pillars of the peat store.

WHAT'S IN A NAME?

The beck which we follow on the outward half of the walk, and which is here referred to as **HARD LEVEL GILL**, in fact assumes no fewer than five different names during its five-mile course from the moors to the Swale at Healaugh. Starting life as **FLINCHER GILL**, it becomes **HARD LEVEL GILL** at Level House Bridge. On passing the smelt mill it can't decide whether to be called **OLD GANG BECK** or **MILL GILL**, and finally, below Surrender Bridge, it kicks both titles into touch and settles for **BARNEY BECK**.

GREAT PINSEAT HAS MANY 'BELL-PITS'
WHERE EARLY MINING OF SURFACE LEAD WAS CARRIED OUT BY 'OPENCAST' METHODS. SHALLOW SHAFTS WERE DUG INTO THE VEIN, AND THE EXCAVATED SOIL FORMED A CIRCULAR MOUND. THE EXAMPLES HERE WERE PROBABLY DUG IN THE MID-18TH C., AND ARE NOW PARTLY FILLED IN AND GRASSED OVER. THE SUMMIT OF PINSEAT IS BEHIND THE WALL (MARKED BY AN O.S. COLUMN). THERE IS NO PATH OR RIGHT-OF-WAY TO IT.

SURRENDER MILL was built c 1840 on the site of an earlier building. There were 2 furnaces, and set

HARD LEVEL FORCE, set attractively in a narrow rocky gorge, is the only picturesque place on the walk, so don't miss it.

between them was the waterwheel which worked the bellows. The 2 flues can be seen, and also the line of the main flue beyond the road.

High on the moor, near a big sheepfold, lie the remains of an old delivery van. Heaven knows where it was going or what it was delivering. This is how it looked in 1989.

MAP O.S. Explorer OL 30 Yorkshire Dales Northern and Central areas.

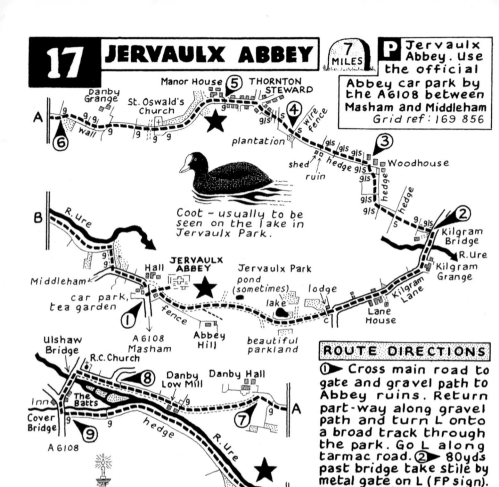

17 JERVAULX ABBEY

7 MILES

P Jervaulx Abbey. Use the official Abbey car park by the A6108 between Masham and Middleham
Grid ref: 169 856

Manor House ⑤ THORNTON STEWARD

Danby Grange

St. Oswald's Church

④

wire fence

plantation

③ Woodhouse

shed ruin

hedge g/s

Coot – usually to be seen on the lake in Jervaulx Park.

R. Ure

JERVAULX ABBEY

Hall

Middleham

car park, tea garden

①

fence

Abbey Hill

A6108 Masham

Jervaulx Park

pond (sometimes)

lake

beautiful parkland

Kilgram Bridge

R. Ure

Kilgram Grange

Kilgram Lane

lodge

②

Lane House

c

Ulshaw Bridge

R.C. Church

The Batts

Inn

Cover Bridge

A6108

⑨

⑧

Danby Low Mill

Danby Hall

⑦

A

hedge

R. Ure

Fish Pond Plantation

B

ROUTE DIRECTIONS

①➤ Cross main road to gate and gravel path to Abbey ruins. Return part-way along gravel path and turn L onto a broad track through the park. Go L along tarmac road. ②➤ 80yds past bridge take stile by metal gate on L (FP sign). Forward along old cart-track to gate, then go straight across field to stile (wm) in hedge. Cross next field to gate at RH corner, then turn R up towards farm. ③➤ Make for large open barn to L of farm, and on reaching it turn L to gate (wm). Keep straight on, with a hedge on your L. ④➤ At far end of small plantation cross stile (wm) in wire fence and go ½ R across field to gated stile (wm). Cross narrow enclosures to gate/stile into walled path. Continue up into village and go L along the main street. ⑤➤ At end of village go through gate (Manor Farm) and down tarmac lane. Cross car park to small gate. Continue along RH edge of two fields, then keep straight on alongside wall on L. ⑥➤ At far end of small plantation go through small gate (blue arrow) and follow top edge of field to gate (wm). ⑦➤ Just before reaching Hall turn L down green cart-track, which eventually becomes a farm road. ⑧➤ Straight on along tarmac road. Turn L at T-junction and L again at main road. ⑨➤ On crossing bridge take swing-gate (FP sign) on L and follow obvious riverside path for 1½ miles. Take gate on R to cart-track up to main road and go L back to car-park.

44

AN EXPLORATION OF THE ATMOSPHERIC RUINS OF ONE OF YORKSHIRE'S GREAT CISTERCIAN ABBEYS IS FOLLOWED BY A DELIGHTFUL AND EASY RAMBLE THROUGH PARKLAND AND PASTURES. THE RETURN IS ALONG THE BANKS OF THE SPARKLING COVER AND THE SEDATE URE. THE WALK IS ALMOST LEVEL, AND YET IS SET AMID UNDULATING WOODED COUNTRYSIDE WHICH PROVIDES SCENERY OF THE VERY HIGHEST QUALITY.

17

Jervaulx Abbey

was founded c 1156 by monks who had forsaken a very bleak establishment near **ASKRIGG** in search of a more hospitable site. Jervaulx grew prosperous from sheep-rearing, and was renowned throughout the country for the breeding of fine horses. The monks also made cheese from ewes' milk — the original **WENSLEYDALE CHEESE**. Disaster struck in 1536, when the abbey's treasures were seized by **HENRY VIII** and the buildings were severely mutilated at the hands of the Crown. The last abbot, **ADAM SEDBAR**, was executed for his part in the **PILGRIMAGE OF GRACE** — a protest against the Dissolution of the monasteries. Very little is left of the great **CHURCH**, which measured 270' by 63', but considerable remains of the **DOMESTIC BUILDINGS** survive.

Pair of arches in the Outer Parlour, leading to the Cloister.

KILGRAM BRIDGE is very ancient - probably pre-Elizabethan. According to local folklore it was built by the Devil in a single night.

✝ The remote **ST. OSWALD'S CHURCH** has traces of pre-Norman work in the walls of the nave. The chancel is mainly Early English, dating from about 1210. Peaceful and beautiful.

DANBY HALL

IS AN ANCESTRAL HOME OF THE **SCROPE FAMILY**, WHICH IN TUDOR TIMES OWNED VAST ESTATES THROUGHOUT UPPER WENSLEYDALE.

At **ULSHAW BRIDGE** be sure to visit the beautiful little **CHURCH OF ST. SIMON AND ST. JUDE**, which was built by the Scropes in the mid-19th C. On the bridge note the **SUNDIAL**, dated 1674. The bridge was once an important river crossing on an ancient York to Kendal route.

Coverbridge Inn

★ COVER BRIDGE ★

At the northern end of this graceful bridge stands a characterful pub much patronised by the angling fraternity. It was a coaching inn in the 16th century, and the bar, with its huge beams, wooden settles and open log fire, has changed but little over the years. The GENTS is dated 1674.

MAP O.S. Explorer 302 Northallerton and Thirsk

18 AYSGARTH & WEST BURTON

6 MILES

P Aysgarth Falls. From the A684, ½ mile E of Aysgarth village, a road goes down to the National Park Centre, Grid ref: 011 887

Large car park (pay and display).
Aysgarth is a 'honeypot', so avoid summer weekends and Bank Holidays.

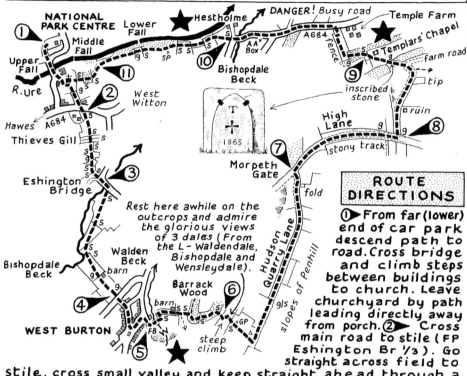

NATIONAL PARK CENTRE — Lower Fall — DANGER! Busy road — Temple Farm
Middle Fall — Hestholme — A684 — Templars' Chapel
Upper Fall — AA Box — farm road — tip
R. Ure — Bishopdale Beck — inscribed stone — ruin
West Witton — 1865 — High Lane — stony track
Hawes A684 — Morpeth Gate — fold
Thieves Gill — ROUTE DIRECTIONS
Eshington Bridge
Rest here awhile on the outcrops and admire the glorious views of 3 dales (From the L - Waldendale, Bishopdale and Wensleydale).
Walden Beck — barn — Hudson Quarry Lane — slopes of Penhill
Bishopdale Beck
Barrack Wood — barn
WEST BURTON — FB — GP — steep climb

ROUTE DIRECTIONS

① From far (lower) end of car park descend path to road. Cross bridge and climb steps between buildings to church. Leave churchyard by path leading directly away from porch. ② Cross main road to stile (FP Eshington Br ⅓). Go straight across field to stile, cross small valley and keep straight ahead through a series of stiles, eventually bearing L down to stile into road. ③ Cross bridge and take stile on R (SP West Burton ¾). Follow clear path across two fields, cross two stiles on river bank, then cross two more fields (passing R of barn). ④ Cross road to path (FP West Burton 75yds). Go R into village then L alongside village green. ⑤ At Mill House turn R. Cross stone bridge and go sharp L up wallside path. Pass R of barn and at wall-corner keep straight on uphill. Enter wood and turn R (SP Hudson Quarry Lane). Follow rising path to leave wood at a stile. ⑥ Climb very steeply to gated stile on skyline. Keep straight on (clear path) up to crosswall and go L along broad green track. ⑦ At track-junction go R. ⑧ Take gate on L into walled track. Descend farm road to a RH hairpin bend, then go L between two plantations and down to fenced ruin. ⑨ Take nearby corner-stile and descend stony track to gate. Turn R to follow fence, then go L along main road. ⑩ Cross bridge and take small gate (FP sign) on R. Cross field diagonally to gateway (wm), then follow obvious riverside path. ⑪ Path eventually bears L to climb alongside ruined wall to stile (wm) at LH end of plantation. Keep straight on through two more stiles to reach churchyard.

AYSGARTH'S FAMOUS FALLS AND THE CHARMING WATERFALL AT WEST BURTON HIGHLIGHT THIS LOVELY WALK IN THE MOST BEAUTIFUL PART OF WENSLEYDALE. THERE ARE SUPERB VIEWS FROM PENHILL'S LOWER SLOPES, WHILST THE URE PROVIDES SOME DRAMATIC RIVER SCENERY. FOR GOOD MEASURE THE ROUTE VISITS THE INTERESTING REMAINS OF A CHAPEL BUILT IN MEDIEVAL TIMES BY THE MYSTERIOUS KNIGHTS TEMPLAR. THERE'S A CLIMB OF SOME 650' – STEEP IN PLACES - FROM WEST BURTON TO HUDSON QUARRY LANE ; ALL THE REST IS EASY GOING.

18

AYSGARTH

owes its fame as Wensleydale's most popular beauty spot to the fact that the URE, for the most part a sedate and somewhat dull river, here achieves a rare turbulence as its foaming waters plunge over a series of broad, rocky steps. Adjacent to YORE BRIDGE (1539) stands a former spinning mill built in 1784 and rebuilt, to twice its size, after being badly damaged by fire in 1853. YORE MILL supplied the red flannel for the shirts of Garibaldi's army. It later became a flour mill, and remained so until 1968. The CHURCH was, from the early Middle Ages, the mother church for the whole of Upper Wensleydale, and at one time Aysgarth was the biggest parish in England. The magnificent SCREEN (c1506) on the south side of the chancel came from Jervaulx Abbey.

✹ DO THIS WALK IN EARLY SPRING, BEFORE THE TREES ARE IN LEAF. IN HIGH SUMMER THE LOWER AND MIDDLE FALLS ARE HIDDEN. ✹

WEST BURTON,
one of the Dales' prettiest villages, has a history reaching back to pre-Domesday times. The excellent Fox and Hounds pub overlooks a spacious green on which the old market-cross steps now support a huge obelisk (1820). Coal was once mined in the area, and lead-mining flourished for 200 years from the late 17thC. The waterfall, E of the village in a wooded dell, is an absolute gem.

TEMPLARS
were members of a military – religious order which was founded in 1118 to protect pilgrims on their way to the Holy Land. Their headquarters were near Solomon's Temple in Jerusalem, and their original and full title was 'Poor Knights of Christ and of the Temple of Solomon'. The order spread throughout much of Europe and became extremely powerful, but was disbanded in the 14th century. The Penhill Preceptory was built c1200 and handed over to the Knights Hospitallers in 1312. Excavations in 1840 revealed the low ruins of a tiny chapel which was, in all probability, part of a larger establishment which remains hidden.

stone coffin, Templar's Chapel

MAP OS Explorer OL 30 Yorkshire Dales Northern and Central areas.

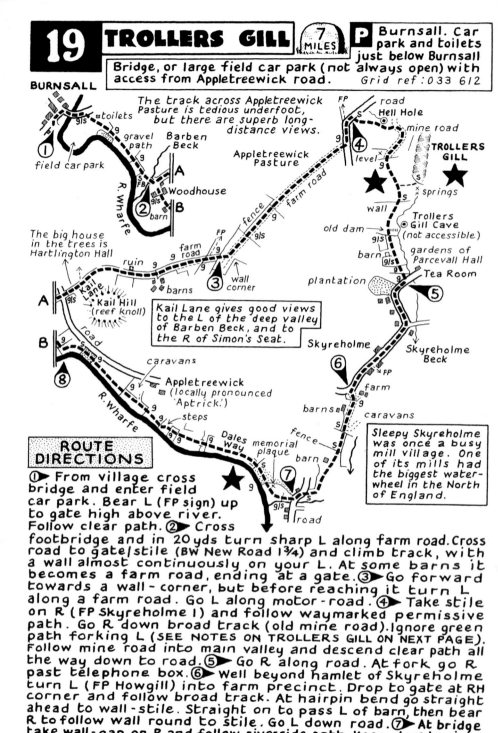

19 TROLLERS GILL

7 MILES

P Burnsall. Car park and toilets just below Burnsall

Bridge, or large field car park (not always open) with access from Appletreewick road.   Grid ref: 033 612

BURNSALL

toilets

g/s

field car park

① gravel path

Barben Beck

R. Wharfe S FB

② Woodhouse A

g/s B

barn

The track across Appletreewick Pasture is tedious underfoot, but there are superb long-distance views.

Appletreewick Pasture

FP road

Hell Hole S

mine road

TROLLERS GILL

④

level

springs

wall

Trollers Gill Cave (not accessible)

old dam g/s

barn g/s

gardens of Parcevall Hall

plantation

Tea Room

⑤

farm road

fence g/s g

farm road

FP g

ruin

Kail Lane

barns

wall corner

③

Kail Hill (reef knoll)

The big house in the trees is Hartlington Hall

Kail Lane gives good views to the L of the deep valley of Barben Beck, and to the R of Simon's Seat.

A g/s

B

road

caravans

Appletreewick (locally pronounced 'Aptrick.')

⑧

R. Wharfe

steps

Dales Way

memorial plaque

barn

Skyreholme

⑥

FP

farm

barns

caravans

fence S

S

Skyreholme Beck

Skyreholme Beck

Sleepy Skyreholme was once a busy mill village. One of its mills had the biggest waterwheel in the North of England.

⑦ S

g/s S

road

ROUTE DIRECTIONS

① From village cross bridge and enter field car park. Bear L (FP sign) up to gate high above river. Follow clear path. ② Cross footbridge and in 20 yds turn sharp L along farm road. Cross road to gate/stile (BW New Road 1¾) and climb track, with a wall almost continuously on your L. At some barns it becomes a farm road, ending at a gate. ③ Go forward towards a wall-corner, but before reaching it turn L along a farm road. Go L along motor-road. ④ Take stile on R (FP Skyreholme 1) and follow waymarked permissive path. Go R down broad track (old mine road). Ignore green path forking L (SEE NOTES ON TROLLERS GILL ON NEXT PAGE). Follow mine road into main valley and descend clear path all the way down to road. ⑤ Go R along road. At fork go R past telephone box. ⑥ Well beyond hamlet of Skyreholme turn L (FP Howgill) into farm precinct. Drop to gate at RH corner and follow broad track. At hairpin bend go straight ahead to wall-stile. Straight on to pass L of barn, then bear R to follow wall round to stile. Go L down road. ⑦ At bridge take wall-gap on R and follow riverside path. Keep close to river; Avoid any paths forking R. ⑧ Path turns R   *Cont. on next page*

48

WHILST THE STARK GRANDEUR OF THE TROLLERS GILL RAVINE IS THE HIGHLIGHT OF THIS EXPEDITION, THE WHOLE WALK IS ENRICHED BY SOME OF THE BEST SCENERY IN MID-WHARFEDALE. THE CLIMBING IS EASY AND GRADUAL, AND LOVELY OLD GREEN TRACKS, PANORAMIC VIEWS AND FINE RIVER SCENERY COMBINE TO PRODUCE A WALK OF GREAT VARIETY AND INTEREST.

19

ROUTE DIRECTIONS cont: at wall. Go forward through farmyard to reach footbridge at point 2. Retrace the outward route.

★

BURNSALL, a charming village, is seen at its best in mid-week; on summer weekends it gets horribly crowded. **ST. WILFRID'S CHURCH** dates in part from the 12th C., and is approached through an unusual 17th C. tapsel gate. Nearby is the **OLD GRAMMAR SCHOOL**, founded by Sir William Craven in 1602 and used as a grammar school until 1876. By the elegant five-arched bridge stands the excellent **RED LION**, formerly the Bridge End Inn. A noggin here will bring the walk to a perfect conclusion.

TROLLERS GILL IS A DRAMATIC LIMESTONE GORGE WITH STEEPLY-OVERHANGING WALLS. THIS IS THE HAUNT OF THE DREADED 'BARGUEST', A SPECTRAL HOUND WITH HUGE, GLARING EYES. IT IS POSSIBLE TO WALK DOWN THROUGH TROLLERS GILL, BUT IT'S AWKWARD AND SLIPPERY - PARTICULARLY IN WET WEATHER. IT IS BETTER BY FAR TO DESCEND THE MAIN VALLEY THEN DETOUR LEFT TO A STILE (ILLUSTRATED) GIVING ACCESS TO THE FOOT OF THE GORGE.

Old level near the mine road. Keep out. All mine levels are potentially dangerous.

WOODHOUSE FARM stands on the site of one of the Dales' lost villages. Here, in monastic times, was a thriving settlement belonging to the Priory of Marton - in - Richmondshire. It is said to be the birthplace of Lord Nelson's grandmother.

PARCEVALL HALL, one of the grandest houses in Upper Wharfedale, is now used as a retreat centre for Bradford Diocese. The beautiful gardens are open to the public.

★

It was once the home of William Nevison, a notorious highwayman.

MAP O.S. Explorer OL 2 Yorkshire Dales Southern and Western areas.

49

20 GAPING GILL

5¼ MILES

P Clapham. Large car park (pay and display) and toilets at top end of Church Avenue.

Grid ref: 745 692

Before setting off, check that you have some loose change to feed the ticket machine at the start of the trail through Clapdale Wood (40p at the time of writing).

GAPING GILL ⑤

Disappointment Pot

Bar Pot ④

☠ **DON'T GO NEAR THE RIM OF GAPING GILL'S SHAFT - A SLIP WILL MEAN CERTAIN DEATH**

Clapham Bottoms shakeholes

wall

Trow Gill ⑥

Foxholes

Beck Head Stream Cave
Clapham Beck Head
Ingleborough Cave ③

ruined wall

The Grotto ✗

Clapdale Wood

Long Lane

Clapham Beck

pens

②

Lake

⑦

Ingleborough Hall

Thwaite Lane

car park

①

CLAPHAM

ROUTE DIRECTIONS

① From car park entrance go R up road. Go L at church, over bridge, then R (SP Ingleborough Cave). ② Go R through gate (SP Ingleborough Cave). Pay at machine to enter woods. Gravel path zig-zags uphill and soon becomes broad track. ③ At Ingleborough Cave go straight on along broad path. Climb through the bouldery Trow Gill and continue alongside wall on L. ④ Cross double ladder-stile and follow clear path. Keep R at fork to head for the fenced crater of Gaping Gill. ⑤ Retrace steps to cross stile at point 4 and head straight away along green path. Ignore a thin path forking R. Path curves L and becomes less clear. Descend towards valley bottom, with big shakeholes close by on L. ⑥ Just past the last shakehole the path divides into three. Take RH path and at path junction turn R up rising green path. Take LH of two gates in crosswall to descend broad, stony track (see NOTE below). ⑦ At junction turn R (BW Clapham ¼). Descend through tunnels to reach church.

NOTE: Although it passes below some impressive limestone scenery, Long Lane itself can be a bit tedious. If you get brassed off with it, you can escape by crossing a step-stile on the R (marked # on the map), descending to a footbridge and re-tracing the outward route through Clapdale Wood.

Have your ticket handy in case someone asks to see it. A short detour L at the church will enable you to see the tunnels.

Clapham Church

THE WALK UP TO GAPING GILL FROM CLAPHAM IS A CLASSIC; A MAGNIFICENT SUCCESSION OF BEAUTIFUL AND AWE-INSPIRING HIGHLIGHTS. APART FROM A VERY SHORT SECTION AT CLAPHAM BOTTOMS THE WALK IS ENTIRELY ON CLEAR PATHS AND TRACKS, BUT IT'S ROUGH UNDERFOOT BETWEEN TROW GILL AND POINT 4. FROM GAPING GILL THOSE WITH A SURPLUS OF ENERGY COULD, ON A CLEAR DAY, EXTEND THE WALK BY POPPING UP INGLEBOROUGH (CLEAR PATH, 3 MILES THERE AND BACK, JUST OVER 1000' OF ASCENT). IN MIST RETURN FROM POINT 4 BY THE TROW GILL ROUTE, AS CLAPHAM BOTTOMS COULD BE CONFUSING.

20

CLAPHAM

is one of the Dales' prettiest and best-loved villages. It was granted a market charter as long ago as 1201; the **MARKET CROSS** opposite the **NEW INN** is a modern shaft in an ancient base. The **OLD MANOR HOUSE**, at the car park entrance, is dated 1701. Until recently it was a National Park Centre. The **CHURCH**, which is surprisingly spacious, retains a splendid 14th C. tower, but was

New Inn

otherwise rebuilt in 1814. The ends of the former Jacobean pews now panel the walls.

HIGHLIGHTS OF THE ASCENT

● **THE LAKE**. Holds about 15 million gallons. Artificial. Constructed c 1833. ● **THE GROTTO**. Elaborate ornamental shelter built early 19th C. to provide employment in a time of recession. ● **INGLEBOROUGH CAVE**. Famous showcave open to public since 1838. Link with Gaping Gill established 1983. Guided tour takes about an hour. An underground experience not to be missed. ● **CLAPHAM BECK HEAD**. Major resurgence of water from Gaping Gill system. ● **BECK HEAD STREAM CAVE**. Low entrance at foot of small scar on L leads into noisy stream passage. ● **FOXHOLES**. Not visible from track. Large entrance up on L (behind big fallen tree), just before track swings L into Trow Gill. Has yielded evidence of Neolithic occupation some 4000 years ago. Now populated by rabbits (and perhaps foxes). ● **TROW GILL**. Spectacular dry limestone gorge with sheer walls some 80' high. Formed by glacial meltwaters at end of last Ice Age. Popular haunt of rock-climbers. ● **BAR POT**. In big rocky hollow (with trees) to L of path. Large rectangular entrance. Don't go in - deep shaft just inside. ● **DISAPPOINTMENT POT**. In funnel-shaped shakehole L of path.

☆
GAPING GILL is the most famous pothole in the country. Here the waters of Fell Beck, on reaching a huge shakehole, plunge into the stark and awesome hole at its base, and fall for 340' before hitting the floor of a huge chamber 110' high, 90' wide and nearly 500' long. A complete descent of this fearsome shaft was first achieved by the French adventurer E.A.Martel in 1895. Since then a vast system of passages has been discovered. Ordinary mortals (walkers) may now make the descent in the relative comfort of a bosun's chair lowered by a winch. This contraption is operated at Spring and Summer Bank Holidays by local potholing clubs. It's an unforgettable experience.

MAP OS Explorer OL 2 Yorkshire Dales Southern and Western areas.

P Settle. Car park and toilets (Pay and Display) * at the N end of town near the viaduct.

Grid ref: 819 638

* 'Pay and Display' refers to the car park, not the toilets!

ROUTE DIRECTIONS

(map labels:) Ingleton, Horton in Ribblesdale; car park, toilets; SETTLE; Albert Hill; Skipton; Malham; allotments; Brockhole Lane forms a section of the National Park boundary; Mitchell Lane; Fish Copy Barn; Houman Laithe; Lodge Farm; tarmac lane; Pond Plantation; Peart Crags; Black's Plantation; wall; Hudsa Plantation; young trees; CLEATOP PARK; FB

① ▶ Walk into the Market Place and bear L along road signposted Upper Settle, Malham, Airton. Pass in front of big, old house (The Folly) and go up Victoria St. ② ▶ Keep R at fork (leaving main road) to proceed along Commercial St. ③ ▶ Just past end of Lower Greenfoot turn L along a rough lane (FP sign). Keep R (straight on) at gated fork. ④ ▶ Cross tarmac lane to stile (FP Mearbeck). Go up to stile in top LH corner, straight on through another, then follow wall on L to pass alongside wood. Go through gap in crosswall and immediately take gate on L to enter wood. Clear path climbs diagonally R. ⑤ ▶ Look for a path coming up from a footbridge on R. Here turn L to follow clear path to wall-stile at top of wood. ⑥ ▶ Descend big field, aiming for wall-corner in front of prominent farm. Follow wall to gate just to R of farm. ⑦ ▶ Go R up farm road. At fork go R up to gate/ladder-stile. Follow broad track past the plantation and into walled lane. ⑧ ▶ Just before reaching another plantation turn sharp L over ladder-stile then turn R (FP Upper Settle). Follow wall on R to stile at bottom of field. ⑨ ▶ Descend the next field, bearing L to gate in front of old wall-stile. Turn R and descend alongside wall. Use gate to cross to other side of wall and follow it down to another gate. ⑩ ▶ Turn L down tarmac lane and follow it back to Settle.

> The rhododendrons in Hudsa Plantation make a colourful show in early summer.

BROCKHOLE LANE is a delightfully leafy and floriferous old byway. The arch of the quaintly named FISH COPY BARN has a keystone inscribed IH 1826. On the climb to CLEATOP PARK there is a fine retrospective view of PENYGHENT. From the stile at the top of the wood one looks across Settle to the green copper dome of the chapel at GIGGLESWICK SCHOOL and the noble profile of INGLEBOROUGH.

Fish Copy Barn

WALKERS LEAVING SETTLE ALMOST INVARIABLY POINT THEIR BOOTS TOWARDS THE GLEAMING, LOFTY LIMESTONE SCARS TO THE NORTH - EAST. THIS DELIGHTFUL LITTLE WALK PROVIDES A MARKEDLY CONTRASTING ALTERNATIVE, TAKING US BY WAY OF FLOWERY GREEN LANES AND PASTURES INTO THE GENTLY UNDULATING, PEACEFUL COUNTRYSIDE TO THE SOUTH OF THE TOWN. BEAUTIFUL WOODLAND AND PANORAMIC VIEWS ALONG AND ACROSS RIBBLESDALE. SOME DOG - WALKERS MAY FIND THE HIGH WALL - STILE AT POINT 6 A BIT AWKWARD.

Ye Olde
Naked Man

SETTLE is a lively little town clinging to the steep hillsides and overlooked by the towering limestone cliffs of CASTLEBERG *(depicted in the sign on the left)*. Recorded as 'Setel' in the Domesday Book, and granted a market charter in 1249, Settle is a fascinating, higgledy - piggledy hotchpotch of narrow alleys, steep lanes and picturesque old courtyards, with here and there some fine Georgian town-houses. In the MARKET SQUARE the prominent, arch-fronted building is called THE SHAMBLES – built in the 17th C. and originally an open market hall. The arches and cottages were added during the late 18th C., and around 1898 the cottages were given an upper storey. Across the Square stands YE OLDE NAKED MAN CAFE, formerly an inn and so named from the relief figure of a man modestly hiding his credentials behind a 1668 datestone. In Victoria Street we pass a huge, Tudor-style house with an ornate central doorway and fine Jacobean windows. Known as THE FOLLY, it was built in 1675 for Thomas Preston, a wealthy tanner (hence the alternative name of Tanner Hall). UPPER SETTLE is the oldest part of the town, and has some very attractive little groups of 17th and 18th century cottages. With its wealth of visitor and tourist amenities Settle is an ideal base from which to explore the magnificent limestone country of the western and southern parts of the Yorkshire Dales.

Albert Hill, Upper Settle

RHODODENDRON

R. ponticum

This shrub was discovered in Eastern Turkey and introduced into Britain in the 18th C., where it was widely planted in open woodland to provide cover for game. Unfortunately it proved to be invasive, spreading rapidly by means of suckers and seeds. R. ponticum is unpopular with foresters, for it monopolises the undergrowth of a wood and, once established, is almost impossible to eradicate.

CLEATOP PARK

Better-known as Cleatop Wood

This patch of ancient and richly colourful woodland is owned by the National Park and designated as a Site of Special Scientific Interest. An extensive range of woodland plants can be found here, and the wide variety of trees includes oak, beech, birch, pine and larch. From the gate at the bottom of the wood there is a fine view across Ribblesdale to Lancashire's dark, heathery Bowland Fells.

MAP O.S. Explorer OL2 Yorkshire Dales Southern and Western areas.

P Pateley Bridge. Long stay car park at far end of Nidd Walk.
Grid ref: 158 654

ROUTE DIRECTIONS ① Walk up High St. and turn L along Church St. Straight on up New Church St. and along Wath Rd. ② Road crosses trackbed of old inclined railway. At far side of bridge cross stile and climb with wall on L. At top turn L to follow path into quarry heaps, where it becomes a broad green track. ③ Go L along tarmac lane and follow it down into valley. At T-junction turn R. ④ Road crosses a stream. Turn R (BW sign) here and climb wide track through wood. At top of wood, when track forks, go L. ⑤ Pass through gate across track and in 150yds turn sharp L through gate (wm). Descend green path, pass end of dam to small gate and follow clear path down valley. ⑥ At road go R over bridge and cross main road to stile. Straight on uphill, pass L of barn and straight ahead across next field to gate/stile. Go ½ L to climb steeply to stile on skyline. ⑦ Pass L of solitary tree and bear slightly L to stile. Keep L of farm buildings, then L along farm road and R along tarmac road. ⑧ At Y-junction go L (BW Foster Beck). Follow farm road. ⑨ At cattle-grid go straight ahead (Nidderdale Way) to LH of two gates (wm). Follow wall on R to gate then drop to barn, where take RH gate and keep straight on. From fence gate head for RH end of farm. Pass L of farmhouse and straight on down field. ⑩ Go L along tarmac road. In 80yds go through gate (wm) on R. Cross bridge, go R up rough track then L between walls. ⑪ Cross footbridge and go L to gate. Pass directly in front of house and follow access road. Turn L along main road. ⑫ Just before

cont. on next page

Gouthwaite Reservoir

flooded quarry
derelict farm
fork L
Spring Wood
R. Nidd

Note the old inscription above the door of this barn

Ī6AδX
WM 8

Inn
⑥ ④
WATH +chapel

Heathfield
Spring Hill
⑧ ⑦
Pie Gill Green
⑨ Leng House (Boys Brigade)
barn
fence
farm
⑩
Bridge Inn and former watermill
⑫ farm
Ashfold Side Beck
caravans
Foster Beck
Mosscar
access road
⑪
Brandstone Beck

Wath Lane
③
fence
excellent green path
former railway (The Incline)
Scot Gate Ash Quarry (dis)
(increasingly steep)

R. Nidd
②
caravans — millions of 'em
①
weir
St. Cuthbert's Church
PATELEY BRIDGE
Recreation Ground
Nidd Walk

The waterwheel

THOUGH NIDDERDALE IS NOT INCLUDED IN THE NATIONAL PARK, THE UPPER PART OF THE VALLEY, ABOVE PATELEY BRIDGE, IS CERTAINLY OF NATIONAL PARK STANDARD. THIS WALK IS SET IN PERHAPS THE PRETTIEST AND MOST SYLVAN SCENERY OF THE DALE. HAVING THREE UPHILL SECTIONS, TWO OF THEM STEEP, THE WALK IS QUITE STRENUOUS. REFRESHMENTS MAY BE ENJOYED AT THE MIDWAY STAGE BY MAKING A SHORT DETOUR L FROM EITHER POINT 4 OR POINT 6 TO THE EXCELLENT SPORTSMAN'S ARMS.

★ **A SOFT OPTION** There's a small car park by Wath Bridge at point 6 (144 677), from where you may take a beautiful short stroll (point 6 to 4 to 5 to 6 — 1½ miles).

ROUTE DIRECTIONS cont : reaching farm take gate/stile on R (FP Pateley Bridge). Cross field to gate and beckside path, which crosses a footbridge and ends at a gate. Bear R to join riverside path back to Pateley Bridge.

PATELEY BRIDGE

was first recorded — as 'Patlea' — in the 12th C. In those days the settlement was in all probability up on the hillside near the now-ruinous St Mary's Church (built 1321 and replaced by St Cuthbert's 1827). Edward II granted a Market Charter in 1320, and in the same year there was the first mention of a bridge. This would have been a wooden structure; the present bridge is 18th C. Pateley Bridge — the capital of Upper Nidderdale — has a good range of shops, restaurants and pubs, and is a very popular holiday centre. The author, who tends to judge a place by the quality of its fish and chips, regards Pateley Bridge as one of his favourite towns.

War Memorial

SCOT GATE ASH QUARRY provided huge gritstone slabs for railway platforms, quays and steps of public buildings. The 300 yd - long INCLINE was built 1871 - 3 to transport stone down to the railway sidings in Pateley Bridge. The quarry closed during World War I.

Be sure to take a peep inside the Methodist chapel at **WATH**. Built in 1859 onto the end of a row of cottages, it's one of the smallest chapels in England. Rudyard Kipling's father regularly preached here. **WATH BRIDGE**, at point 6, was used as a packhorse bridge by the monks of Fountains Abbey.

GOUTHWAITE RESERVOIR

WAS CONSTRUCTED 1895 - 1901 ON THE SITE OF A FORMER GLACIAL LAKE. THE MASSIVE 80' HIGH DAM HAS CREATED THE BIGGEST OF ALL YORKSHIRE'S RESERVOIRS, WITH A SURFACE AREA OF 332 ACRES. GOUTHWAITE ATTRACTS MANY WADING BIRDS AND WATERFOWL, ESPECIALLY IN WINTER, AND IS THUS A MECCA FOR BIRD-WATCHERS. BETWEEN 1950 AND 1971 183 BIRD SPECIES WERE RECORDED HERE.

SURE

B B

STEADFAST

Boys' Brigade insignia, Leng House

THE WATERMILL was a working flax mill until 1966 before being converted into an inn, which has now been re-converted into apartments. The magnificent wheel, which is of 1904 vintage, boasts a diameter of 35 feet, making it one of the largest 'overshot' water-wheels in the country.

MAP O.S. Explorer 26 Nidderdale

23 OLD COTE MOOR & LITTONDALE

6¼ MILES

P Kettlewell.
Car park (pay and display) behind garage at S entrance to village.
Grid ref: 968 723

TAKE CARE – steep, rocky, awkward and slippery

OLD COTE MOOR

KETTLEWELL

car park, toilets

easier going

ridge wall

Penny Pot

Nickle Pot GP

Spr

GP

Byre Bank Wood

crumbling wall

highest point of walk 1610'

The Slit

broad path

wall

R. Wharfe

R. Skirfare

wall

GP

bank erosion

barn

fence

wall

LITTONDALE

Hawkswick

ruined wall

superb green path in bracken

Knipe Scar

ridge wall

ARNCLIFFE

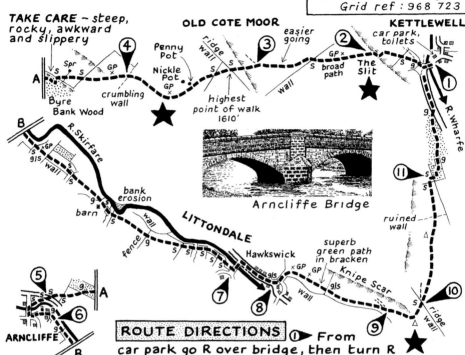

Arncliffe Bridge

ROUTE DIRECTIONS

① From car park go R over bridge, then turn R and take LH of two gates (FP Arncliffe). In 50yds fork L (FP Arncliffe) to climb steep path. Pass through narrow cleft in limestone scar. ② Head directly away from Kettlewell on a faint path which soon becomes a broad green track. Cross a ladder-stile. ③ On nearing a low scar fork L up a thinner path. Climb scar to ladder-stile in ridge-wall. Continue along broad path. ④ After crossing a crumbling wall the path descends to a ladder-stile into a wood. Descend steep, rocky path to gate at bottom of wood, then descend, on a R diagonal, two fields to roadside stile. ⑤ Cross road to stile (FP sign). Follow wall on L to another roadside stile. Go L over bridge. At road junction keep L (but detour straight on to visit village). In 50yds go L through stone gateposts (FP Hawkswick) and along drive. Keep L of The Vicarage Cottage. ⑥ Follow yellow-topped marker-posts and continue along riverside path. Path is not always visible, nor always close to river, but the route, through many stiles and gates, is obvious. ⑦ Cross big footbridge and go R along road. ⑧ At far end of village turn L (FP Kettlewell) up rough track to gate/stile. Go straight on uphill between walls, then follow RH wall as it swings R. Follow broad green path through bracken. ⑨ When it turns sharp L go straight on up flagged path. At a cairn path swings L up to ladder-stile. ⑩ Two paths head away from stile. Take either. At a cairn path bears R and descends towards a wood. ⑪ Cross ladder-

cont. on next page

THE STEEP CLIMB AT THE OUTSET OF THIS WALK GIVES A FINE RETROSPECTIVE BIRD'S - EYE VIEW OF KETTLEWELL. PASSING THROUGH A NARROW CLEFT IN THE LIMESTONE SCAR, THE ROUTE RISES MORE GENTLY OVER OLD COTE MOOR BEFORE DESCENDING TO THE PRETTY VILLAGE OF ARNCLIFFE. AFTER A STROLL BY THE BANKS OF THE SKIRFARE, THERE ARE MORE SUPERB VIEWS FROM KNIPE SCAR. THE WALK IS STRENUOUS (BY J. KEIGHLEY STANDARDS), WITH THE TWO CLIMBS OVER THE MOOR TOTALLING JUST OVER 1,500' OF ASCENT. NOT A GOOD DOGGIE - WALK (TOO MANY LADDER - STILES).

ROUTE DIRECTIONS cont: stile into wood and descend clear path. Enter small enclosure, keep R of ruin, then L past a wall - corner to a gate. Descend woodland path (at fork take either) and go L along road back to Kettlewell.

KETTLEWELL

This little grey village, with its splendid old cottages clustered around the beck, nestles in a hollow at the foot of Great Whernside, Wharfedale's highest mountain at 2,310'. Kettlewell was a thriving market town as long ago as the 13th C. During the 18th and 19th centuries it became a lead-mining centre. There are three excellent pubs (there used to be 19!). The Blue Bell dates back to 1680, and the Racehorses was once the Blue Bell's stable block. The King's Head also dates to the 17th C., and was once a workhouse.

PENNY POT is a small rift in a shakehole immediately to the R of the path. In wet weather a tiny stream sinks into it.

★

NICKLE POT lies just beyond, in a deep shakehole in the heather about 40 yds to the R of the path.

★

BYRE BANK WOOD is a patch of ancient woodland which has probably survived because of its steep gradient. Botanists will find much of interest here.

LITTONDALE

is Wordsworth's 'Amerdale' and Kingsley's 'Vendale'. It is a U-shaped glacial valley drained by the Skirfare, a river with a habit of disappearing underground. In Norman times it was a hunting forest, before becoming a huge sheep-rearing estate of the wealthy Fountains Abbey. Littondale is one of the very few dales unscarred by the ravages of lead-mining. It is noted for its superb field barns, and is a birdwatcher's paradise.

◄ ARNCLIFFE ►

The major settlement of Littondale is an attractive little village of mellow cottages grouped around a spacious green which sports a stone water-pump of mid-19th C. vintage. Arncliffe was the first setting for the soap opera 'Emmerdale Farm' (now just 'Emmerdale'), and the delightfully old-fashioned Falcon Inn was the original 'Woolpack'.

ST. OSWALD'S CHURCH occupies a site on which a stone church has stood since c1100. About 1500 this church was partially demolished and rebuilt; only the tower remains. Inside the church is a list of Littondale men who fought in 1513 in the Battle of Flodden Field.

carved heads, Arncliffe Church

MAP O.S. Explorer OL 30 Yorkshire Dales Northern and Central areas.

24 INGLEBOROUGH 5¼ MILES

ROUTE DIRECTIONS

P Chapel-le-Dale. Triangular hardstanding by the B6255 Hawes-Ingleton road 300yds NW of the Hill Inn. Grid ref: 746 778

① Go R down road. Just past small building take gate on L (BW Great Douk ⅝ FP Ingleborough 2⅜) and follow cart-track to gate/ladder-stile. Cross next field, heading directly towards Ingleborough, to gate/ladder-stile. ② Turn L up green path to reach walled, wooded crater of Great Douk. A stile provides access to a steep, slippery path descending RH side of crater. ③ Return to stile and follow clear path around LH side of crater. Pass fenced pothole up on your L and head for prominent gate in wall, with Ingleborough directly beyond. Maintain direction across next field to gated stile in crosswall, then go straight on alongside wall on R. ④ Turn L up flagged path. ⑤ When flagstones end continue up a very steep, rocky path. At the top go through swing-gate and follow clear path up ridge to summit (O.S. column and wind-shelter). ⑥ Retrace route of ascent, taking EXTREME CARE on the steep section, to double-stile at end of flagged path. Before crossing, however, you may turn L to detour for about 200yds, bearing slightly L, to locate Sunset Hole. The two cave entrances (wet and dry) are at the far side of a patch of clints. Return to cross double-stile and descend broad path, passing L of huge shakehole. Ignore any paths forking R. ⑦ Below the scar the path swings R to contour the hillside. Ignore path forking L downhill. Keep straight on to rejoin outward route at point 2.

! The section between point 5 and the ridge is hair-raisingly steep and demands extreme care — especially in descent. Dangerous in icy or very windy conditions.

*

Take some spare warm clothing — even on a hot summer's day it can be bitterly cold at the summit.

*

In mist the vast summit plateau can be very confusing. Be sure to take a compass.

*

If the ascent is not feasible, a very pleasant 2 or 3 hours can be spent pottering around the lower slopes searching out potholes.

*

58

ALTHOUGH NOT THE HIGHEST DALES'
MOUNTAIN, INGLEBOROUGH IS EASILY THE
MOST-ASCENDED, FOR IT RISES IN SPLENDID
ISOLATION IN THE VERY HEART OF LIMESTONE
COUNTRY, AND ITS BOLD OUTLINE IS A GREAT
CHALLENGE TO WALKERS. THIS IS THE SHORTEST OF THE
THREE POPULAR ROUTES TO THE SUMMIT, AND IT UTILISES
A SPLENDID FLAGGED PATH WHICH HAS BEEN EXPERTLY
LAID ACROSS THE NOXIOUS SWAMPS OF HUMPHREY BOTTOM.
BETWEEN POINTS 2 AND 4 AN 'OFF-THE-BEATEN-TRACK'
ALTERNATIVE TO THE MAIN PATH VISITS SOME FASCINATING
CAVES AND POTHOLES, INCLUDING THE SPECTACULAR
GREAT DOUK CAVE. STRENUOUS – 1,400' OF ASCENT.
BEFORE SETTING OFF, PLEASE READ THE DIRE WARNINGS
AT THE FOOT OF THE PREVIOUS PAGE.

INGLEBOROUGH

The OLD HILL INN is immensely popular with walkers and potholers.

was once thought to be the highest mountain in England. On its vast summit plateau the Brigantes built a huge fort as a defence against the Romans ; sections of the 13' thick perimeter wall still remain. The cruciform wind-shelter has a view-indicator (above eye-level so easily missed) atop its central column. A pile of masonry near the western escarpment is all that remains of a hospice tower built in 1830. To the east of the wind-shelter you may be able to discern the circular foundations of the ancient Brigantian huts.

PLAN OF SUMMIT

our route

A summit cairn
B O.S. column
C wind-shelter
D remains of hospice
E fort perimeter wall
F hut circles

CAVES AND POTHOLES

GREAT DOUK CAVE is at the base of a huge, tree-lined crater. A stream emerges in a waterfall from the cave and sinks into the crater's bouldery floor. About 100yds south of Great Douk, and a little to the L of the path, is the fenced rift of LITTLE DOUK POT, a 40' vertical shaft into Great Douk Cave. MIDDLE WASHFOLD CAVES are located in an isolated outcrop by a sheepfold. Two streams flow into the system – one immediately behind the north end of the fold and another south of the fold, whilst there are several dry entrances among the clints. All these passages unite, and the water emerges at Great Douk Cave. The prosaically named P97a is a sinkhole with some magnificently fluted limestone blocks. SUNSET HOLE has two entrances – one dry and one wet. The wet entrance is illustrated L. They unite after a few yards and may be entered by a 'novice' with a good torch and explored for some distance – with the probability of getting wet feet. LOWER SUNSET can be found in a small rocky hollow just below the track, and is part of the same system.

BRAITHWAITE WIFE HOLE, 65yds in diameter and over 90' deep, must be a serious contender for the title of 'The Dales' Biggest Shakehole'.

MAP O.S. Explorer OL2 Yorkshire Dales Southern and Western areas.

25 FLASBY FELL 5½ MILES

ROUTE DIRECTIONS

① ▶ Go through gate (BW Flasby 2½) and along vehicle track. ② ▶ 120yds past second cattle-grid fork R (BW sign) up well-trodden green path. The shapely cone of Sharp Haw soon comes into view, and the ridge-path to its summit is obvious. From summit (O.S. column) bear R down through gap in wall and descend clear path to gate in crosswall. ③ ▶ Bear ½ L to follow clear path (blue-topped marker-posts). Path through high bracken keeps close to wood on L, descending steeply to gate. Forward with wall on L then descend walled track. ④ ▶ At farm on R turn L (SP Stirton) along farm road. Keeping R of all buildings it ends at a field gate. ⑤ ▶ Old cart-track winds up field to gate. Continue up woodland track. ⑥ ▶ When track forks go R. In 20yds fork L along narrow path through rhododendrons. ⑦ ▶ Turn L up forest road and follow it for nearly two miles. It leaves the plantation at a gate/stile before descending to rejoin the outward route at point 2.

P Stirton. From the B6265 Grassington to Skipton road about ½ mile N of the Craven Heifer Inn take a narrow, unsignposted lane leading SW to Stirton. At the first sharp bend there is a gate on the R marked 'PRIVATE ROAD'. There is room here to park 4 cars CONSIDERATELY. (On the author's last visit – a Bank Holiday Monday – there were 14 vehicles parked here – some of them obstructing the lane). Grid ref: 975 539.

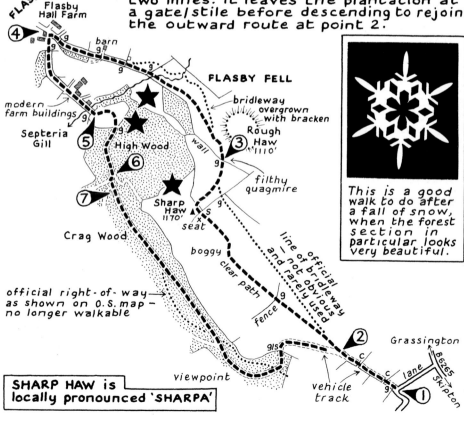

FLASBY

Flasby Hall Farm

④

barn

FLASBY FELL

modern farm buildings

bridleway overgrown with bracken

Septeria Gill

⑤

High Wood

wall

③ Rough Haw 1110'

⑥

filthy quagmire

⑦

Crag Wood

Sharp Haw 1170'

seat

boggy

line of official bridleway – not obvious and rarely used

official right-of-way as shown on O.S. map – no longer walkable

clear path

fence

② Grassington

viewpoint

vehicle track

lane

B6265 Skipton

①

This is a good walk to do after a fall of snow, when the forest section in particular looks very beautiful.

SHARP HAW is locally pronounced 'SHARPA'

THIS PLEASANT RAMBLE AT THE SOUTHERN EDGE OF THE NATIONAL PARK CLOSE TO THE 'GATEWAY TO THE DALES' TOWN OF SKIPTON OFFERS A RICH VARIETY OF TERRAIN AND SCENERY INCORPORATING FOREST ROADS, FARM LANES AND COLOURFUL BRACKEN-CLOTHED FELLSIDES. THE WALK, WHICH IS ACCOMPLISHED WITHOUT SETTING FOOT ON TARMAC, IS ON CLEAR PATHS AND TRACKS, BUT CAN BE MUDDY. THE PATH UP THE SOUTH-EAST RIDGE OF SHARP HAW IS HUGELY POPULAR WITH LOCAL DOGS, WHO LOVE TO EXERCISE THEIR OWNERS HERE.

25

FLASBY FELL

is the general name for the upland triangle between Skipton, Gargrave and Hetton, and takes its title from the tiny hamlet on the Gargrave - Hetton road. It has two named summits, Sharp Haw and Rough Haw, whilst north of these are two lesser heights.

Looking back to Rough Haw from the descent to Flasby Hall Farm.

SHARP HAW

is very prominently in view on the approaches to Skipton and Grassington from the south. It is the summit of a long ridge, and appears in views from most directions as a graceful peak. The ridge is heavily forested on its western and northern slopes. An OS column adorns the summit.

ROUGH HAW

may be reached by a short, steep detour from the gate at point 3. It's not an official right-of-way, but then again nor are several other sections of this walk. Rough Haw's flat top has a small cairn and a cosy, hollowed-out wind-shelter. From the eastern edge of the summit plateau there is a fine view across the valley to the gritstone edges of Barden Moor. The monument above Cracoe, the cross above Rylstone and the ruins of Norton Tower can all be seen. The top of Rough Haw is a delectable place for a siesta on a hot summer's afternoon.

Flasby Hall Farm

CONIFER PLANTATIONS

can sometimes seem rather gloomy and oppressive, but they provide an ideal habitat for birds such as CROSSBILL, SISKIN, GOLDCREST, COAL TIT, JAY, WOODPECKER, LONG-TAILED TIT AND LONG-EARED OWL. The tiny ROE DEER are denizens of conifer forests, where their numbers have increased in recent years.

MAP | O.S. Explorer OL 2 Yorkshire Dales Southern and Western areas.

26 SEMER WATER

P Marsett, a small village 1 mile SW of Semer Water.

Use roadside verges by bridge at entrance to the village. Take care not to obstruct any farm access.

Grid ref: 903 862

The three minor dales radiating beyond Marsett are (L-R) Cragdale, Raydale and Bardale.

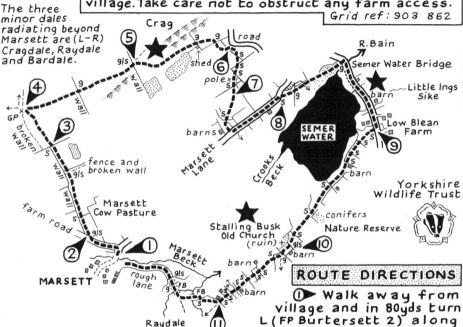

ROUTE DIRECTIONS

① ▶ Walk away from village and in 80yds turn L (FP Burtersett 2) along walled farm road. ② ▶ In 200yds take gate/stile (wm) on R and climb alongside wall on L. ③ ▶ When wall ends keep straight on uphill. Thin path eventually bears L to guidepost. ④ ▶ Turn sharp R along path which runs clear and level to gate in crosswall. Continue along broad path, rising slightly to gate/stile in another crosswall. ⑤ ▶ Path bears slightly R and descends, winding below crags and passing through two gates. ⑥ ▶ Through gap in wall and immediately (before reaching road) turn R down field to stile in wall on R. Go diagonally L to gated stile, then maintain direction past a telegraph pole to a stile by a solitary tree. ⑦ ▶ Maintain direction down steep hillside to stile near farm buildings. Go L down to gate then L up road. ⑧ ▶ In about ⅓ mile take fence-stile on R (FP Semerwater Bridge ¼). Descend to gate in crosswall. Forward with wall on L, then keep straight on through trees to gate. Go R along road. ⑨ ▶ At farm take gate/ladder-stile on R (FP Stalling Busk 1¼). Go straight ahead on level path, passing through a series of stiles. ⑩ ▶ At ruined church bear slightly L to gate. Fork R (SP Marsett) to follow clear path through another series of stiles. ⑪ ▶ From stile adjoining corner of barn go R across field, over wall-stile and L to footbridge. Just beyond it turn R along cart-track. Cross another footbridge and follow the track to Marsett.

MARSETT is a tiny farming community. It's little Wesleyan chapel was built in 1897. 'Sett' is a common suffix to place names in this part of Wensleydale. It comes from the Old Norse 'sætre', meaning a lowland farmstead.

A CIRCUIT OF THE LARGEST NATURAL LAKE IN THE DALES. THE WALK BEGINS WITH A CLIMB OF 850' – QUITE GRUELLING ON A HOT DAY – FROM MARSETT TO THE RIDGE AT POINT 4, BUT THERE IS AMPLE REWARD – A BRACING HIGH-LEVEL MARCH WITH LOVELY VIEWS OF THE LAKE REFLECTING THE SURROUNDING COUNTRYSIDE. THE RETURN IS AN EASY STROLL ALONG GENTLE FIELD PATHS, VISITING THE LAKE SHORE AND A TINY, FASCINATING RUINED CHURCH IN AN IDYLLIC SETTING, BUT THE PROFUSION OF STILES WILL NOT BE TO EVERYONE'S LIKING.

26

SEMER WATER

The distinctive, flat-topped hill 1½ miles east of the lake is ADDLEBROUGH (1564')

★

The RIVER BAIN is claimed to be the shortest river in England. From Semer Water it flows for just two miles before joining the Ure at Bainbridge.

★

The CARLOW STONE, an enormous boulder near the lake shore, is said to have been a missile hurled by a giant at the Devil.

THE DALES' LARGEST NATURAL LAKE IS BUT A REMNANT OF A LARGER GLACIAL LAKE FORMED SOME 8,000 YEARS AGO. IT IS STILL, HOWEVER, A CONSIDERABLE SHEET OF WATER, WITH A SURFACE AREA OF 90 ACRES, A CIRCUMFERENCE OF 1½ MILES AND A MAXIMUM DEPTH OF 45'. SEMER WATER IS A SANCTUARY FOR WINTER WILD-

The Carlow Stone

FOWL AND A HONEYPOT FOR SUMMER CROWDS, ATTRACTING WIND-SURFERS, CANOEISTS, YACHTSMEN AND ANGLERS. THE LAKE HAS A LEGENDARY 'SUNKEN CITY,' THE STORY OF WHICH IS TOLD IN SIR WILLIAM WATSON'S POEM 'BALLAD OF SEMERWATER'. THE LEGEND MAY HAVE A FACTUAL BASIS ; LAND RECLAMATION WORK IN 1937 UNCOVERED THE REMAINS OF A PREHISTORIC LAKE VILLAGE, WHICH COULD HAVE BEEN DESTROYED BY A SUDDEN FLOOD.

STALLING BUSK OLD CHURCH

A stile provides access to the atmospheric ruins of this tiny church. Built c 1602, it was badly damaged during the Civil War (1642-9), and was re-built in 1722. Some of the stones from the original church were used in the rebuilding. The church remained in use until 1909, when a new church (St. Matthew's) was built in the hamlet. The interior arcades of the old church run N-S rather than the usual E-W. About 750 people lie at rest in the churchyard.

A 'Creep Hole' or 'Cripple' in a wall allows sheep to pass between fields. There are good examples near two of the stiles on this walk.

MAP O.S. Explorer OL 30 Yorkshire Dales Northern and Central areas.

7¼ MILES

P Reeth. Park in village centre (small charge – honesty box) Grid ref: 037 993

ROUTE DIRECTIONS ①▶

Leave Reeth by the Richmond road. 150 yds past bridge take gate on R (FP Grinton ½). ②▶ Follow riverside path, then marker-posts, then bear L through gate and on to Grinton Bridge. ③▶ Go across bridge to visit church (not to be missed), then go back over bridge and turn sharp R onto riverside path. ④▶ Just before reaching fence-stile into open field take wall-stile on L. Follow wall on R to stile, then up to gate. Cross tarmac lane to stile. ⑤▶ Go ½ R, climbing gently to gate/stile in fence 60yds below wood. Take a level course through a series of stiles. Approaching Priory keep R of fence. ⑥▶ Pass L of Priory/farm buildings. Cross cattle-grid and take gate on L (SP Marrick ¾). Climb green path to small gate and follow flagged path up through wood to gate/stile. Keep straight on, with wall on R. ⑦▶ At road-junction turn L and go straight on up tarmac lane. ⑧▶ At T-junction take facing stile (FP sign) and cart-track up to gate. Walk alongside wall on L (broad path) for 1¾ miles. ⑨▶ Cross fence-stile (wm) and take gate on L. Descend rough track, which eventually develops into a tarmac lane. ⑩▶ Pass a fingerpost (BP Arkendale 4) on your R, and 80yds beyond it go R down walled path. ⑪▶ Turn R along tarmac lane, and in a few yards take path on R to gate/stile. Follow wall on L, cross it at a narrow stile and cross fields to Reeth Bridge.

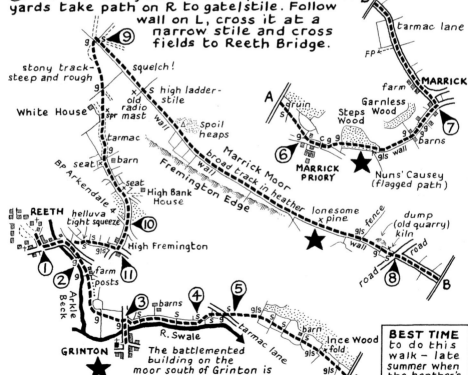

stony track-steep and rough

squelch!

White House

old radio mast

high ladder-stile

spoil heaps

tarmac

barn

BP Arkendale

seat

seat

High Bank House

Fremington Edge

wall

Marrick Moor broad track in heather

lonesome × pine

tarmac lane

FP

farm

MARRICK

Garnless Steps Wood Wood

A

ruin

MARRICK PRIORY

Nuns' Causey (flagged path)

barns

gls wall

B

dump (old quarry) kiln

road

road

fence

wall

REETH

helluva tight squeeze

Arkle Beck

farm posts

High Fremington

GRINTON

barns

R. Swale

tarmac lane

barn

Ince Wood fold

★ The battlemented building on the moor south of Grinton is GRINTON LODGE, a 19th C shooting lodge. It has been a Youth Hostel since the 1940s.

BEST TIME to do this walk – late summer when the heather's in bloom.

A WALK OF INFINITE VARIETY WHICH TAKES US THROUGH RIVERSIDE MEADOWS AND HILLSIDE WOODS AND PASTURES AS A PRELUDE TO AN EXHILARATING MARCH ALONG THE EDGE OF A HEATHER · CLAD MOOR. FROM THIS AIRY VANTAGE POINT THE SWEEPING VIEWS OF SWALEDALE, AND THE PROSPECT OF REETH NESTLING AT THE FOOT OF LOVELY ARKENGARTHDALE, ARE QUITE EXCEPTIONAL. THE CLIMB OF ABOUT 850' FROM THE PRIORY TO THE MOOR TOP IS LONG AND GENTLE; THE DESCENT PAST WHITE HOUSE IS STEEP AND ROUGH UNDERFOOT. A TALL LADDER · STILE ON THE MOOR MAY BE A PROBLEM FOR DOG - WALKERS.

27

One of Reeth's many tea shops

REETH *rejoices in a beautiful setting at the confluence of Arkengarthdale and Swaledale, and is a perfect base from which to explore each of these lovely valleys. A market charter was granted in 1695, and in the 18th and 19th centuries Reeth was an important lead-mining centre. Since the cessation of mining activities Reeth's population has dwindled to about a quarter of its former size, but nevertheless it is regarded as the 'capital' of Upper Swaledale, and the many inns, cafés and shops around the huge sloping green still retain an air of prosperity. At the lower end of the green is a small National Park Centre. The Swaledale Folk Museum displays exhibits illustrating the fascinating local history.*

Morning Shadows

GRINTON CHURCH

IS AN ABSOLUTE GEM. IT WAS BUILT BY MONKS FROM BRIDLINGTON ABBEY IN THE EARLY 12TH C. THERE'S AN ORIGINAL NORMAN WINDOW ABOVE THE TOWER ARCH, BUT THE PRESENT BUILDING IS LARGELY 15TH C. THE CHURCH HAS A NORMAN FONT, A JACOBEAN PULPIT AND A BOOKSTAND SO OLD THAT IT MAY WELL HAVE BEEN USED BY THE MONKS. IN THE S WALL IS A 'LEPER'S SQUINT' (ILLUSTRATED R) THROUGH WHICH PEOPLE WITH CONTAGIOUS DISEASES COULD WATCH THE SERVICE.

MARRICK PRIORY was founded c 1154 as a house for Benedictine nuns. It is now a residential youth activity and field study centre, and is a rather odd jumble of church, farm and domestic buildings, with a few fragments of ancient ruins here and there. The priory was unusual in that it was left undamaged during the Dissolution of Monasteries in 1536. The flagged path known as the Nuns' Causey has over 300 steps, and leads up towards the village of Marrick, which lies at 1000'.

The lonesome pine.

This is the old radio mast above Fremington Edge as it looked in 1990. Since then the top half of the mast has fallen down, and the little building has vanished.

MAP O.S. Explorer OL 30 Yorkshire Dales Northern and Central areas.

28 THE DRUID'S TEMPLE

5 MILES **P**

The Druids' Temple is not easy to find. It lies in Druids' Wood, to the W of the Ilton to Healey road. Look for a lane (on the L if driving towards Healey) with a signboard 'SWINTON ESTATE WOODLANDS'. At the end of this lane (beware potholes) is a car park which you may use by kind permission of the Earl of Swinton.

Grid ref : 177 786

DANGER. RISK OF FIRE. Do not light fires or discard cigarette ends.

LOCATION MAP

HIGH ELLINGTON
A6108
FEARBY
HEALEY   MASHAM
CP   SWINTON
ILTON   A6108
Druids   R.Ure
Temple
Leighton
Reservoir
moor road   GREWELTHORPE
to Lofthouse (Nidderdale)
KIRKBY   Ripon→
MALZEARD

ROUTE DIRECTIONS

①▶ Through metal gate and take LH track. ②▶ At 'crossroads' (stone blocks on central 'island') turn L down to gate (viewpoint). Return to stone blocks and go straight on to follow the main track past Temple and back to car park. Straight on down access lane. ③▶ Take stile (wm) on L. Follow powerline. Through gate, then go L alongside plantation to gate. Follow cart-track down to gate/ladder-stile. ④▶ Go ½ L across big field, aiming towards buildings on distant hillside. Cross fence-stile (wm) and maintain direction. ⑤▶ Just before end of next field double back sharp R to follow clear path alongside woodland. Keep straight on along an old tractor trail, then pass R of farm and along farm road. ⑥▶ Straight on along tarmac road. At junction keep straight on (Swinton 1½). Cross ford and continue uphill. ⑦▶ Just past ford warning sign take stile (wm) on R. Climb to gate (wm) in fence and straight on across next field to gate (wm). Follow path through woodland to stile. ⑧▶ Negotiate 'tricky bit' (see WARNING on next page). Pass ruin on your L and follow clear path along valley, with stream to your R. Ignore fence-stile (wm) on your R. ⑨▶ At large barn turn L up road and in a few yards take track on R. Follow track alongside plantation. ⑩▶ At crosswall go through gate (NOT stile on its L). Turn R and climb to farm. Go L around buildings and out along farm road. Turn L up lane to return to car park.

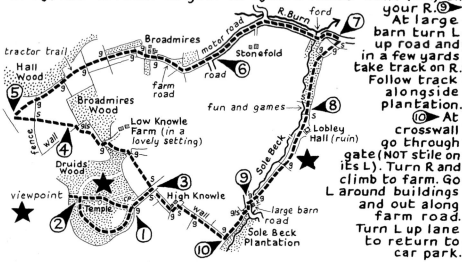

R.Burn   ford   ⑦
Broadmires
motor road   Stonefold
tractor trail   ⑥
Hall   road
Wood
farm   fun and games ▶ ⑧
road
⑤   Broadmires   Lobley
Wood   Hall (ruin)
fence   wall   Low Knowle
Farm (in a   Sole Beck
lovely setting)
④   Druids   ⑨
Wood   ③   large barn
viewpoint   High Knowle   road
★   Temple   wall   Sole Beck
② ①   ⑩   Plantation

WELL-CONCEALED IN THE HEART OF A WOOD SOME THREE MILES SW OF MASHAM LIES AN INTERESTING MOCK-ANTIQUITY KNOWN AS THE DRUID'S TEMPLE. THIS IMPRESSIVE AND FASCINATING STRUCTURE IS THE HIGHLIGHT OF A SHORT, PEACEFUL STROLL IN THE GENTLY UNDULATING WOODED COUNTRYSIDE ON THE EASTERN FRINGE OF THE YORKSHIRE DALES.

WARNING There's a problem at point 8 in that the wallside path has collapsed into the stream. At the time of writing (Oct 04) it was just about possible for an agile person to scramble up between wall and stream, but it seems likely that further erosion will eventually put paid to that option. The alternative is to ford and re-ford the stream, and with this in mind you should EITHER a) do the walk in wellies OR b) pop a couple of plastic bin-liners into your rucksack. Avoid doing this walk after heavy rain, when the stream may be in full spate.

PLAN OF TEMPLE

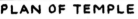
looking out

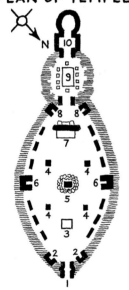

The entrance and the inner guards

William Danby, landowner, of Swinton Hall, organised the construction of this mock temple c1820 to provide work for local tenants and estate employees at a time of widespread unemployment. He paid them a shilling a day. The structure, a scaled-down copy of Stonehenge, is oval in shape, and all its stones are still standing. Scattered around the wood are a number of other stone constructions which are components of the overall plan. The Temple is considered to be England's best druidical folly.

• —●— •

Ring-necked pheasant

THERE ARE SO MANY PHEASANTS HEREABOUTS THAT IT IS QUITE AN ACHIEVEMENT TO COMPLETE THE WALK WITHOUT TRIPPING OVER ONE. THE PHEASANT, A NATIVE OF CHINA AND MONGOLIA, WAS FIRST RECORDED IN ENGLAND IN 1059. IT RELIES ON ITS MOTTLED PLUMAGE AS CAMOUFLAGE, BUT EVEN SO IS VULNERABLE TO FOXES, WEASELS, STOATS AND OTHER PREDATORS. 10-15 OLIVE-GREEN EGGS ARE LAID BETWEEN APRIL AND JUNE, AND TAKE ABOUT 25 DAYS TO HATCH. THE SHOOTING-SEASON BEGINS 1ST OCTOBER.

1 THE OUTER GUARDS
2 THE INNER GUARDS
3 SACRIFICIAL ALTAR
4 THE FOUR COLUMNS
5 THE PHALLUS
6 THE WARDENS OR PRIESTS
7 THE MASTER OR HIEROPHANT
8 THE TWO GUARDS OF THE SOLAR TEMPLE
9 THE SOLAR TEMPLE
10 THE TOMB
Based on an original plan by P.T. Runton Esq.

MAP O.S. Explorer 26 Nidderdale (all but a tiny section).

29 SIMON'S SEAT

7¼ MILES

P Barden Bridge, just off the B 6160 Bolton Abbey to Burnsall road.
Grid ref: 052 574

ROUTE DIRECTIONS

① Through gate and head downstream, with river on your R. Passing L of aqueduct, path runs through woodland high above river, eventually emerging onto tarmac lane. Go R along it. ② At Waterfall Cottage take small gate on L (SP Valley of Desolation) to broad, rising track. After crossing a footbridge it climbs through a plantation and straight on up the moor. ③ Track swings L across head of ravine. ④ At fork go R along rough, bouldery, cairned path, passing R of crags and on towards summit. ⑤ Just before reaching summit rocks note a surfaced path going L. Climb R to summit O.S. column (rock scramble - take care) then return to follow surfaced path. It becomes rough before descending steeply R between walls. Follow broad track downhill.

cont. below L

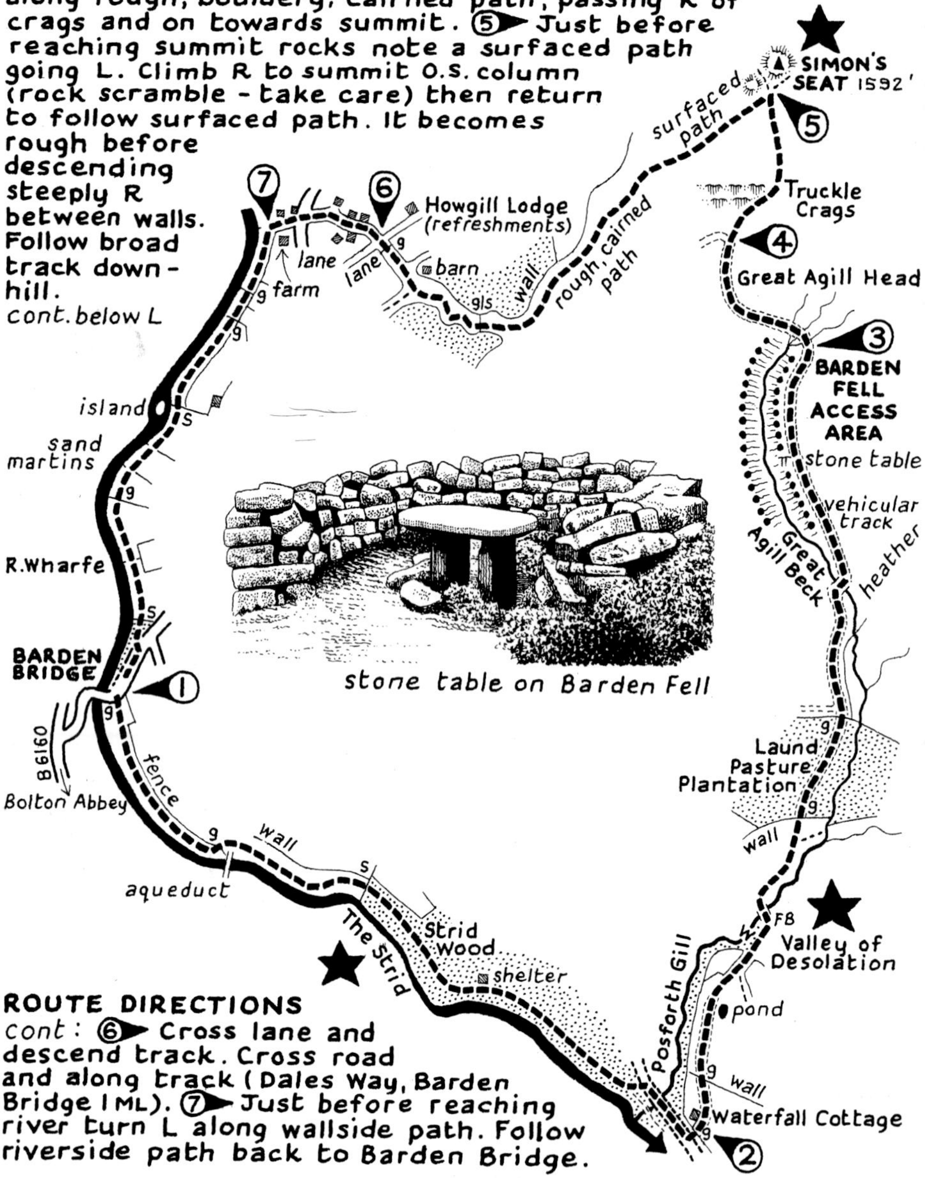

SIMON'S SEAT 1592'
surfaced path
5
Truckle Crags
4
Great Agill Head
3
BARDEN FELL ACCESS AREA
stone table
vehicular track
Great Agill Beck
heather
7
6
Howgill Lodge (refreshments)
lane
lane
farm
barn
gls
wall
rough, cairned path
g
island
s
sand martins
R.Wharfe
BARDEN BRIDGE
1
B6160
Bolton Abbey
fence
wall
aqueduct
The Strid
Strid Wood
shelter
Laund Pasture Plantation
wall
FB
Valley of Desolation
Posforth Gill
pond
wall
Waterfall Cottage
2

stone table on Barden Fell

ROUTE DIRECTIONS

cont: ⑥ Cross lane and descend track. Cross road and along track (Dales Way, Barden Bridge 1 ML). ⑦ Just before reaching river turn L along wallside path. Follow riverside path back to Barden Bridge.

SET IN WHAT IS ARGUABLY THE LOVELIEST PART OF WHARFEDALE, THIS SUPERB WALK HAS JUST ABOUT EVERYTHING — BEAUTIFUL WOODLAND, HEATHER-AND BRACKEN-CLAD MOORS, A FINE ROCKY SUMMIT WITH A GLORIOUS VIEW AND RIVER SCENERY RANGING FROM THE SERENE TO THE SPECTACULAR. THE ASCENT IS LONG AND GRADUAL; THE DESCENT TO HOWGILL IS SHORT AND STEEP. CLEAR TRACKS AND PATHS MAKE THE WALK SAFE IN MIST, BUT FOR MAXIMUM ENJOYMENT IT SHOULD BE DONE ON A CLEAR DAY.

ACCESS AREA

BARDEN FELL is closed on certain days (never Sunday) for shooting, and also in times of drought. Access Point notice boards (there's one at Waterfall Cottage) give information, as does the Estate Office (Tel: 01756 718000) DOGS ARE NOT ALLOWED IN THE ACCESS AREA.

NO DOGS

BARDEN BRIDGE displays, on its parapet, an inscription stating that it was repaired at the charge of the whole of the West Riding in 1676. 'Barden' is Anglo-Saxon for 'Valley of the Wild Boar.'

The aqueduct, built by Bradford Corporation to carry water from the Nidderdale reservoirs.

Waterfall Cottage

☆ **THE STRID** is where the broad waters of the Wharfe are squeezed to a width of about 5' to rush through a deep and notoriously dangerous rock channel. Many lives have been lost here.

☆ **THE VALLEY OF DESOLATION** is so named because of the utter devastation caused by a violent storm in 1826. 'Valley of Desolation' is now a misnomer; this is one of the loveliest places in the Dales.

SIMON'S SEAT

THE SUMMIT IS AN IMRESSIVE GRITSTONE OUTCROP. ON A CLEAR DAY IT'S AN EXCELLENT VIEWPOINT, WITH THE PANORAMA SWEEPING AWAY FROM THE MOORS OF CENTRAL LANCASHIRE IN THE WEST TO THE WHITE HORSE OF KILBURN FAR AWAY TO THE EAST. TO THE NORTH THERE IS A DRAMATIC BIRD'S-EYE VIEW OF THE VALLEY AROUND APPLETREEWICK, AND NORTH-WEST, AMONGST THE TREES, IS THE ANCIENT PARCEVALL HALL AT THE FOOT OF TROLLERS GILL.

These moors make an ideal habitat for many species of bird, providing them with nesting sites, cover and food supplies. Illustrated are the RING OUZEL, which is like a blackbird with a white crescent on its throat, and the SHORT-EARED OWL, whose 'ears' are not ears at all. Please remember that during the breeding season (April to June) disturbance may cause nests to be abandoned and chicks to die.

MAP O.S. Explorer OL 2 Yorkshire Dales Southern and Western areas.

30 PENHILL 6½ MILES

P West Witton. Large layby on A684 just to E of village.
Grid ref: 067 885

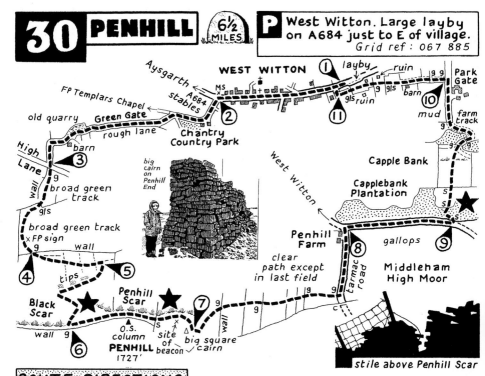

WEST WITTON — layby — ruin — Park Gate
Aysgarth — MS — A684 stables — gls ruin — barn — (10)
FP Templars Chapel — (1) — (11) — mud — farm track
old quarry — Green Gate — rough lane — (2) — Chantry Country Park
High Lane — barn — (3) — Capple Bank
wall — broad green track — big cairn on Penhill End — Capplebank Plantation
gls — broad green track — West Witton — Penhill Farm — (8) — gallops — (9)
×FP sign — wall — clear path except in last field — Middleham High Moor
(4) — tips — (5) — tarmac road
Black Scar — Penhill Scar — (7) — Middleham High Moor
wall — O.S. column — site of beacon — big square cairn
(6) — PENHILL 1727'

stile above Penhill Scar

ROUTE DIRECTIONS

(1) Walk through village. (2) At old milestone (Hawes 13) turn L along tarmac lane, which soon begins to climb. Ignore turnings to R (Templars Chapel) and L (Chantry Country Park). Lane becomes a rough track. (3) At T-junction with walled lane take facing gate. A broad green track climbs the hillside, passing through two fields to reach open moor at a gate. (4) Turn L along clear path. When it forks keep R along level path across plateau. Path crosses fragmentary remains of three old walls. (5) 50yds past the third of these turn R. Thin, clear path soon swings R to pursue a level course along the top of a line of tips. Just past last tip path turns sharp L alongside shallow gully, and soon becomes a sunken path zig-zagging up to gate in ridge-wall. (6) Don't use gate. Turn L to follow wall as far as O.S. column, then bear L to join path along edge of escarpment, eventually curving R to reach a big square cairn (illustrated above). (7) Descend steeply L to join clear path heading L to gate in wall. Go straight on down ridge, passing through a series of gates and gateways. Turn L along road. (8) At junction by farm you have options. Go L for quick return by road to West Witton. (This might be preferable in wet weather, when the route in the vicinity of Park Gate can be abominably muddy). For full walk go R (Middleham 5). (9) In a good ½ mile take slit-stile on L (FP West Witton 1¼). Descend path (stepped in places) to stile at bottom of wood. Down next field to gated stile. Go straight on down big field, eventually bearing slightly R to join a farm track. Follow it down to farm. (10) 100yds past farm take gate on L and follow track. When it peters out keep straight on through a line of gates and stiles. (11) Gate/stile on R gives access to road near layby.

THE HIGHLIGHT OF THIS WALK IS THE DRAMATIC VIEW FROM THE RIM OF THE CRAGS FORMING PENHILL'S NORTHERN FACE. A CLEAR DAY IS THEREFORE ESSENTIAL FOR MAXIMUM ENJOYMENT OF THIS VIGOROUS HIKE OVER WENSLEYDALE'S BEST-KNOWN HILL. THE FIRST HALF OF THE WALK, TO POINT 6, INVOLVES A CLIMB OF JUST OVER 1200'. THE FINAL DESCENT VIA THE WOODED SLOPES OF CAPPLE BANK LENDS A LITTLE VARIETY TO A WALK WHICH IS OTHERWISE PREDOMINANTLY OVER OPEN, EXPOSED UPLAND TERRAIN.

WEST WITTON,

an ancient and attractive village, was once inhabited by craftsmen and lead- and coal-miners who worked on the moors between Wensleydale and Swaledale. **ST. BARTHOLOMEW'S CHURCH** stands on a site once occupied by a Saxon church; the oldest parts of the present building (tower and north wall) date from c1100. Extensive restoration work in 1875 uncovered the remains of a Saxon cross in the church wall. One of the windows depicts the arms of Jervaulx Abbey. The village is perhaps best-known for a quaint old tradition. On the nearest Sunday to St. Bartholomew's Day (Aug 24) villagers chant a rhyme as they march along the street carrying an effigy of 'Owd Bartle', who is then ceremonially burned à la Guy Fawkes. There are conflicting theories as to the origin of Owd Bartle, the most popular claiming that he was a thief who stole swine from Jervaulx Abbey.

The Rhyme of Owd Bartle

At Penhill Crags
he tore his rags;
At Hunter's Thorn
he blew his horn;
At Capplebank Stee
he brak his knee;
At Grisgill Beck
he brak his neck;
At Wadham's End
he couldn't fend;
At Grass Gills End
they made his end;
Shout, lads, shout.

St. Bartholomew's West Witton

RACEHORSES from the many stables around Middleham are put through their paces on MIDDLEHAM HIGH MOOR.

PENHILL

stands in splendid isolation, its huge triangular bulk bounded by Wensleydale (north), Walden (west) and Coverdale (south-east). The O.S. column does not occupy the highest point, for the true summit lies about a mile across the moor to the SW. A small mound marks the site of a beacon and (reputedly) the grave of an Iron Age chieftain.

MAP O.S. Explorer OL 30 Yorkshire Dales Northern and Central areas.

31 CAVES & POTHOLES OF BIRKWITH

7¼ MILES

P

High Birkwith. Leave Horton in Ribblesdale by the lane between the Crown Hotel and the bridge. Pay parking fee at High Birkwith Farm and continue up rough track. Look out for cart track turning up R and park on grass at junction.

Grid ref: 804 772

ROUTE DIRECTIONS

① Go up branch cart-track to gate/stile, but before using it detour R to view Birkwith Cave. A stile provides access. Return to gate-stile, and on using it turn R off cart-track. Skirt fence at head of ravine and maintain level course, with big limestone blocks on L. ② On approaching a small ravine descend R to cross it by ladder-stile and footbridge. Climb R to come alongside wall, then bear L to join a clear, level path. Follow it for a good mile, crossing several ladder-stiles, to reach a barn. ③ Go L up to stile, then R to gate and Sell Gill Holes. About turn and follow broad, stony Pennine Way track for 1¾ miles. ④ Through gate and turn L (PW sign). Follow constructed path past building and alongside wall on L. ⑤ At farm turn R (PW sign) along broad track. ⑥ To omit Ling Gill section, and reduce walk to 5 miles, take ladder-stile on L (just before reaching a barn) and descend past Browgill Cave directly to point 10. For full walk follow Pennine Way to Ling Gill Bridge. ⑦ Cross bridge, turn sharp L downstream then go R alongside wall. ⑧ At ruined barn take ladder-stile on L (FP Nether Lodge ⅞). Descend by wall on L to fence-stile. Bear slightly R down next field to fence-stile in corner (easily missed). Follow wall on L over hill to farm. ⑨ Through farmyard, go L to cross bridge then L to gate/stile. Go R up cart-track (FP High Birkwith). Cross God's Bridge (cave taking stream under track). ⑩ For detour to Browgill Cave (not to be missed) turn L to climb alongside wall on your L. Return to track and follow it (wall on your R) to gate/stile. Stay with cart-track and turn L up road, or take a short-cut over the hill.

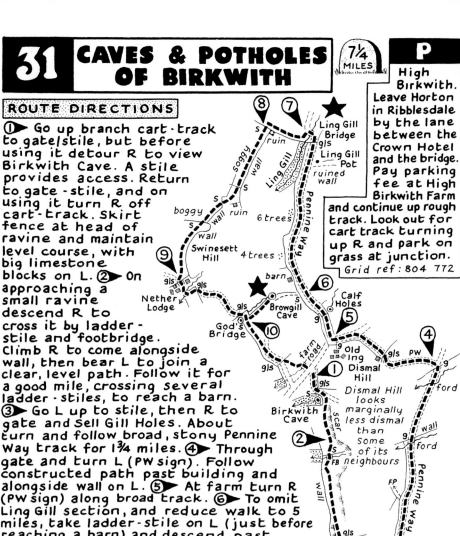

72

SET IN THE VERY HEART OF 'THREE PEAKS COUNTRY,' THE BIRKWITH AREA, A FAVOURITE HAUNT OF CAVERS, ABOUNDS WITH INTERESTING NATURAL FEATURES. THE WALK TAKES US THROUGH PLEASANT LIMESTONE SCENERY, AND FOLLOWS THE PENNINE WAY ALONG OLD PACKHORSE ROADS TO VISIT A MAGNIFICENT GORGE. THE SECTION BETWEEN LING GILL BRIDGE AND NETHER LODGE CAN BE SOGGY.

DANGER! OF ALL THE CAVES AND POTHOLES SHOWN ON THE MAP, ONLY BROWGILL CAVE IS SAFE TO ENTER. SOME ARE PALPABLY DANGEROUS.

BIRKWITH CAVE is a low, wide resurgence cave at the head of a wooded ravine. Very impressive after heavy rain.

Birkwith Cave

The barn at point 3

SELL GILL HOLES

THE WET ENTRANCE IS JUST ABOVE THE TRACK, AND SWALLOWS A SMALL STREAM. JUST BELOW THE TRACK, AT THE END OF A SMALL GULLY, IS THE DRY ENTRANCE — A DANGEROUS 25' SHAFT. BOTH LEAD TO A MASSIVE CAVERN SECOND IN SIZE ONLY TO GAPING GILL.

● JACKDAW HOLE is a huge, tree-fringed crater. ● COWSKULL POT occupies a rocky shakehole identified by its rowan tree. Its main shaft is 70' deep. ● PENYGHENT LONG CHURN lies just beyond Cowskull, about 100 yds from the track. It's a classic Dales pothole, with a stream plunging down a 90' shaft. ● CANAL CAVERN is a narrow rift at the trackside and leads to a 30' pitch into a stream. ● CALF HOLES, very popular with cavers, is a spectacular rocky stream sink. ● LING GILL POT is a small slot 20 yds R of the track in a dry streambed just beyond an info. board. The sound of an underground waterfall can be heard.

Browgill Cave

● GOD'S BRIDGE is a 60' long 'through' cave where Brow Gill flows under the track. Don't be tempted to walk through it - it's full of deep pools. ● BROWGILL CAVE is one of the finest in the district and, when the water-level is low, may be safely explored for about 70 yds. The stream passage can be followed (by experts) to Calf Holes.

LING GILL

THIS WOODED LIMESTONE GORGE IS ONE OF THE MOST DRAMATIC RAVINES IN THE YORKSHIRE DALES. HERE CAM BECK SWIRLS AND CASCADES THROUGH A CHAOTIC JUMBLE OF HUGE BOULDERS, WHILST ABOVE THIS MAELSTROM NEAR-VERTICAL WALLS OF ROCK RISE TO SOME 200'. IT IS A NATIONAL NATURE RESERVE, BUT IS NOT OPEN TO THE PUBLIC DUE TO ITS DANGEROUS SLOPES. WITHIN THE GORGE IS PRESERVED MUCH OF THE NATURAL VEGETATION OF THE LIMESTONE FELLS. THE STURDY OLD GRITSTONE PACKHORSE BRIDGE HAS AN INSCRIBED TABLET (NOW SCARCELY DECIPHERABLE) INFORMING US THAT THE BRIDGE WAS REPAIRED IN 1765 'AT THE CHARGE OF THE WHOLE WEST RIDEING'.

Ling Gill Bridge

NETHER LODGE WAS ONCE A GRANGE OF FURNESS ABBEY.

The Birkwith area is notable for its many **DRUMLINS** — small rounded hills all about 80' high. They are mounds of boulder clay smoothed by the ice which flowed over them 15,000 years ago.

MAP O.S. Explorer OL 2 Yorkshire Dales Southern and Western areas.

32 CATRIGG FORCE & VICTORIA CAVE

5½ MILES

P Langcliffe. Car park at far end of village from main road, near church and school. *Grid ref: 822 650*

ROUTE DIRECTIONS

① Leave car park by narrow lane at its corner. In 50 yds, at Hope Hill Farm, fork R along walled track. Follow it to its end at a gate. ② Follow path alongside wall on R. Climb steep hillside, veering L up to gate at top LH corner. ③ Straight on uphill, past a cairn and into field with outcrops. Cross gate/step-stile (FP sign) on L and climb field to stile. Go R along farm road. ④ Cross cattle-grid and straight on, with wall on L. As cart-track bears R fork L along a thin path to a gate/ladder-stile. ⑤ Descend to gate/ladder-stile at LH corner and immediately take gate on R (SP Catrigg Force). Path zig-zags down to gate and woodland path down to waterfall. Return to gate/ladder-stile at point 5 and go straight on along cart-track. Turn R along tarmac road. ⑥ Cross cattle-grid and go L up broad green path. Beyond a ladder-stile fork L up to another ladder-stile (Jubilee Caves are directly ahead). ⑦ Go R along cart-track for a few yards then fork L up to small gate and wallside path. ⑧ Turn L off path to climb to Victoria Cave, then return to main path. ⑨ At foot of long descent go R through wall-gap to follow broad path. ⑩ When path forks go R. ⑪ At wall-corner keep straight on (towards Settle). Descend steeply by broken wall then turn R along wallside path. Go through gate. ⑫ Go L over ladder-stile (or use gate 20 yds further on). Keep to LH side of field, pass to R of wood (gate) and follow obvious path back down to Langcliffe.

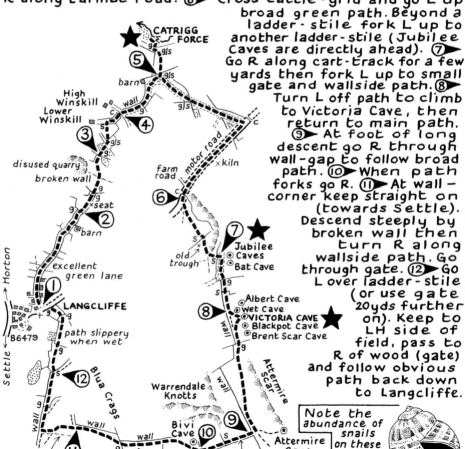

Note the abundance of snails on these scars

74

ON GOOD PATHS AND TRACKS THROUGHOUT, THIS IS A WALK OF EXCEPTIONAL BEAUTY AND INTEREST. NO DALES WATERFALL HAS A LOVELIER SETTING THAN CATRIGG FORCE, PLUNGING 60 FEET INTO A DEEP, WOODED RAVINE. THE MODERATELY STRENUOUS ROUTE PASSES THROUGH SOME WILD AND RUGGED LIMESTONE SCENERY, AND BELOW THE WHITE CRAGS AND SCARS THERE ARE FASCINATING CAVES TO EXPLORE

32

DANGER YOU ARE MOST STRONGLY WARNED NOT TO GO INTO VICTORIA CAVE OR NEAR TO THE ENTRANCE. THERE HAVE BEEN SERIOUS ROCK FALLS. THE AUTHORITY ACCEPTS NO RESPONSIBILITY FOR ANY INJURY OR DAMAGE.

LANGCLIFFE

is a tranquil place now, but has seen more turbulent times. The original medieval settlement, which belonged to Sawley Abbey and stood about ½ a mile N of the present village, was destroyed by marauding Scots in 1318. Langcliffe Hall, an elegant mansion, has a splendid doorway dated 1602, though the house itself is not as old as that. Look out for a house bearing a tablet displaying a naked woman – with a 1660 date strategically positioned. Perhaps she was the girlfriend of Settle's more famous but equally bashful naked man.

CATRIGG FORCE or 'Foss' *

plunges in two steps into a deep pool, and is mightily impressive after heavy rain. The best view is obtained by descending a path to the bottom of the ravine. The area around the top of the fall is dangerous ; definitely not a place for larking about.
* 'Force' is Dales dialect for waterfall from the Norse 'Foss'.

JUBILEE CAVES

There are three entrances – the two illustrated and another round to the R. Excavations within the caves have unearthed remains of numerous Iron Age burials. Most of the skeletons were found secreted in recesses along the sides of narrow inner passages ; one was wearing a necklace made from the teeth of a wolf. **BAT CAVE** is a 10' cave at the foot of a scar 60 yds to the R.

VICTORIA CAVE

WAS SO NAMED BECAUSE IT WAS DISCOVERED IN 1837, THE YEAR OF VICTORIA'S CORONATION. THE HUGE ENTRANCE (40' HIGH AND 100' WIDE) IS ARTIFICIAL – THE RESULT OF EXTENSIVE EXCAVATIONS WHICH HAVE UNEARTHED A WEALTH OF ARCHAEOLOGICAL REMAINS, INCLUDING THE BONES OF GRIZZLY BEAR, REINDEER, HYENA, RHINOCEROS, HIPPO, ELEPHANT AND WILD OX. SOME OF THESE BONES WERE ESTIMATED TO BE AT LEAST 120,000 YEARS OLD.

ATTERMIRE CAVE can be reached by a steep climb-cum-scramble from point 9. With two good torches one can follow a winding passage for 20 yds. If you have more bottle (or less sense) than the author, you can then crawl for 20' into a big chamber containing a knee-deep pool.

MAP O.S. Explorer OL 2 Yorkshire Dales Southern and Western areas.

33 WILLANCE'S LEAP

5½ MILES

P Richmond. From the main Reeth road, near the W edge of the town, drive up Westfields. Park on the verge just before reaching a gate marked 'High Leases'. BE SURE NOT TO OBSTRUCT GATE OR LANE. Grid ref: 153 015

The road walking between points 3 and 4 is not unpleasant, being downhill and with lovely views into Clapgate Gill.

ROUTE DIRECTIONS

① Go through 'High Leases' gate and along drive. Through another gate and in 20yds take stile (wm) on R. Climb steep field, bearing L to pass above large patches of gorse. Beyond gorse keep L to come alongside fence on L and follow it to corner-stile. ② Follow well-trodden path, with fence on R and wooded scar on L. Approaching the monument the fence is replaced by a wall. Keep below it. Path eventually swings R and joins motor-road at a cattle-grid. ③ Turn L and follow road for about a mile. ④ Take gate on L (sign-West Applegarth) and follow farm road. Pass to R of farm. ⑤ Just beyond farm take stile (wm) on R (near a ruin). Turn L to pass alongside the ruin and forward on a level course through two stiles (with 'Coast to Coast' signs). Cross farm road to another 'Coast to Coast' stile and continue forward across two more fields (via a stile (wm) near a trough). ⑥ Turn R along a farm road. In a few yards take gate/stile on L and turn R to walk parallel with farm road to a gate. ⑦ Bear L along broad green path, passing a 'Coast to Coast' guidepost. At a gate/stile the path enters woodland, where it becomes a sometimes muddy track. On emerging from the wood the track continues straight ahead to High Leases and the car.

There are some fine **YEWS** below Applegarth Scar — massive, rather squat trees with gnarled and fluted trunks and foliage of rich dark green which appears almost black from a distance. The pinkish-red 'berries' are properly called arils, for they are cup-shaped and do not completely enclose the seeds, which lie at the base of the cup. The seeds are poisonous, as also are the leaves and the bark. Yews have a life-span of about 1,000 years, and were once regarded as a symbol of everlasting life – which explains why so many are found in churchyards. The wood of yew was, until the 17th C., used for making longbows.

A POPULAR AND EASY WALK IN THE RICHLY COLOURFUL COUNTRYSIDE IMMEDIATELY UP-DALE FROM THE ANCIENT AND FASCINATING TOWN OF RICHMOND. THE OUTWARD ROUTE TRAVERSES THE EDGE OF A LONG LIMESTONE SCAR, FROM WHERE THE VIEWS, BOTH INTO SWALEDALE AND EAST ACROSS THE VALE OF MOWBRAY, ARE TRULY MAGNIFICENT. THE RETURN IS ALONG THE WOODED SLOPES BELOW THE SCAR. IN WET WEATHER THE NARROW PATH BETWEEN POINT 2 AND THE MONUMENT CAN BE VERY SLIPPERY - CARE NEEDED.

33

1606

HEAR US:
GLORY BE TO OUR
MERCIFUL GOD
WHO MIRACULOUSLY
PRESERVED ME FROM
THE DANGER SO GREAT
—o—
THIS STONE WAS RENEWED
AD 1815
GEORGE SMITH ESQ MAYOR
—o—
AND
AGAIN RENEWED AD 1883
PETER CONSTABLE
MAXWELL ESQUIRE
MAYOR
—o—

WILLANCE'S MONUMENT

One foggy day in the autumn of 1606 Robert Willance, a local man from Richmond, was out with a hunting party when his horse took fright, bolted, and leapt over the edge of Whitcliffe Scar. The fall of some 200 feet resulted in the death of the horse, but the rider miraculously survived, suffering nothing worse than a broken leg. Two monuments commemorate the incident and record Willance's thanks to God. He also gave a silver chalice to the town.

In spring and early summer the hillside between High Leases and Whitcliffe Wood is ablaze with **GORSE** - a spectacular and quite unforgettable sight.

THE ROAD ALONG WHICH WE PROCEED BETWEEN POINTS 3 AND 4 WAS THE MAIN RICHMOND TO REETH ROAD PRIOR TO 1836, WHEN THE NEW ROAD WAS BUILT. IT ALSO SERVES AS THE NATIONAL PARK BOUNDARY, WHICH AT POINT 3 TURNS SOUTH ALONG DEEPDALE AND CUTS ACROSS OUR ROUTE AT THE FIRST STILE AFTER POINT 5.

This shapely white cairn stands beside the farm track below Applegarth Scar.

From point 4 onwards we are following The Master's footsteps, for this is a section of Alfred Wainwright's famous 'Coast to Coast' walk from St. Bees Head to Robin Hood's Bay.

| MAP | O.S. Explorer 304 Darlington and Richmond. |

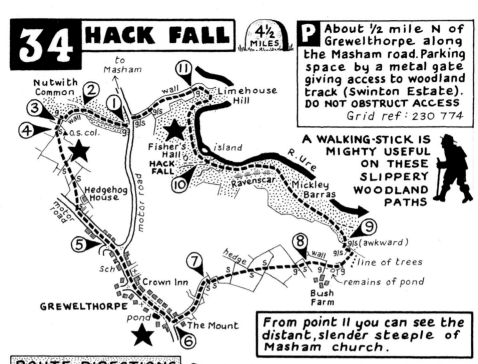

34 HACK FALL

4½ MILES

P About ½ mile N of Grewelthorpe along the Masham road. Parking space by a metal gate giving access to woodland track (Swinton Estate). **DO NOT OBSTRUCT ACCESS**
Grid ref: 230 774

to Masham

Nutwith Common

Limehouse Hill

Fisher's Hall
HACK FALL

island

R.Ure

Ravenscar
Mickley Barras

Hedgehog House

motor road

A WALKING-STICK IS MIGHTY USEFUL ON THESE SLIPPERY WOODLAND PATHS

gls (awkward)
line of trees

hedge
remains of pond

Sch
Crown Inn

Bush Farm

GREWELTHORPE
pond
The Mount

From point II you can see the distant, slender steeple of Masham church.

ROUTE DIRECTIONS ①▶ Start up woodland track (FP sign). ②▶ Where wall on L and track part company follow wall, turning R at a wall-corner to reach a small gate. ③▶ Climb steep field, bearing slightly L to gap at corner, then follow hedge forward for 50yds to stile. ④▶ Cross field to stile 20yds R of powerline. Maintain direction across two more fields to stile in corner. Go L along road. ⑤▶ At road junctions follow 'Ripon' signs to pass through Grewelthorpe. ⑥▶ At far end of village turn L through gate into green lane (immediately L of bungalow called 'The Mount'). Follow main track, ignoring branches to R and L. ⑦▶ At end of green lane take stile (wm) on R and turn L alongside hedge (holly) to corner-stile (wm). Go ½R across field to stile (wm), then ½ L to stile (wm) in hedge. Bear R to stile (wm) about 60yds from field corner. Cross big field to gate (wm) at its far LH corner, then cross narrow field to a stile (wm) in hedge. ⑧▶ Go R to reach gate (wm) at bottom corner of field (well to L of farm). Cross top end of next field. At a former pond (hollow filled with bulrushes) go L (wm). Descend field, with line of trees on your R. At last tree turn L to pass through two stiles (wm) and into woodland. ⑨▶ Clear, level path soon becomes boggy and slippery. It stays at high level for some distance before gradually descending to river, passing below the high crags of Ravenscar (on your L). ⑩▶ Detour L up flight of stone steps, or nearby path, to visit ruined pavilion (Fisher's Hall). Resume on riverside path. It eventually swings L, away from river, and climbs to come alongside a wall. ⑪▶ On leaving the wood, at a gate, keep straight on, climbing the RH side of a very long field. From a gate/stile at the top an enclosed track leads up to the road near the parking place.

TAKE GREAT CARE NOT TO START A FIRE IN THESE WOODLANDS

TWO MILES BELOW MASHAM THE URE PLUNGES AND CASCADES THROUGH A DEEP, DENSELY WOODED GORGE. HERE, RISING OVER 300 FEET FROM THE RIVER'S WEST BANK, IS THE HUGE AMPHITHEATRE KNOWN AS HACK FALL, ONCE A FAMOUS LANDSCAPED GARDEN. THIS WALK, WHILST APPEALING PRIMARILY TO THOSE WHO ENJOY WANDERING THROUGH WOODS, ALSO TRAVERSES SOME PLEASANT FIELD PATHS AROUND GREWELTHORPE. THE PATHS IN HACKFALL WOODS BEING ROUGH, BOGGY AND SLIPPERY, THE WALK IS BEST DONE IN KEEN, FROSTY CONDITIONS OR DURING A LONG, DRY SUMMER SPELL (ADMITTEDLY A RARE PHENOMENON). PROGRESS MAY BE IMPEDED BY FALLEN TREES AND BRANCHES.

34

The O.S. column at the top of Horsepasture Hill is unusually sited beneath a large tree. The earthworks here mark the site of an Iron Age hill fort.

GREWELTHORPE

has a history going back well beyond Domesday times, and may have Roman connections; in the early 20th C. the skeleton of a Roman soldier was unearthed near here. The bones were re-interred in Kirkby Malzeard churchyard, and the soldier's sandals were put on display in York Museum. In the 19th C. Grewelthorpe had several industries, including tanning, straw-hat making and the production of wool and cheese. The excellent Crown Inn is an old coach-house built in 1624. The large and picturesque village pond was probably once a gravel pit ('grewel' is an old word for gravel). Living contentedly here amongst the large colony of resident ducks are coot and moorhen. The former is the one with the white 'shield' on its forehead (hence the saying 'bald as a coot'). The shyer moorhen has a red bill and a white stripe along its flanks. A lovely place to eat your sandwiches - mind the ducks don't pinch 'em!

sign by the pond

Moorhen

Coot

HACK FALL

IN THE 18TH C THE WOODLAND WAS TRANSFORMED INTO A LANDSCAPED GARDEN BY WILLIAM AISLABIE, OF STUDLEY ROYAL FAME. THE PROJECT WAS ON A GRAND SCALE, WITH FOLLIES AND MOCK RUINS, GROTTOES, ROCK WALKS AND ARTIFICIAL PONDS AND WATERFALLS. NATURE AND TIME HAVE TURNED HACK FALL BACK INTO A WILDERNESS; THE ONLY RELIC YOU WILL SEE IS A RUINED OCTAGONAL PAVILION. THIS IS FISHER'S HALL, NAMED IN HONOUR OF WILLIAM FISHER, THE HEAD GARDENER WHO SUPERVISED THE GARDEN'S CREATION. ITS WALLS ARE SURFACED WITH TUFA, A ROUGH TEXTURED LIMESTONE. BIRDLIFE ABOUNDS IN THESE WOODLANDS - LOOK OUT PARTICULARLY FOR THE GREAT SPOTTED WOODPECKER. IN SPRING THE WOODS ARE CARPETED WITH BLUEBELLS AND RAMSONS.

Fisher's Hall

MAP | O.S. Explorer 26 Nidderdale

35 CAPPLESTONE GATE

5½ MILES

P Two roads connect Grassington and Kettlewell - the main B6160 via Kilnsey and, on the E side of the river, a narrow lane via Conistone. It is from the latter that the walk begins, and the suggested parking place is a small roadside recess about a mile from Kettlewell, just below Scargill House. The recess has two field gates (which must not be obstructed), a seat and a footpath sign (Moor Gate 1½ M).   Grid ref : 976 708

In case of difficulty, an alternative would be to park at Conistone (see next page).

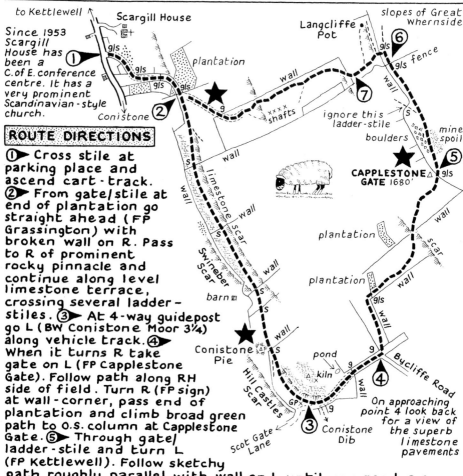

Since 1953 Scargill House has been a C. of E. conference centre. It has a very prominent Scandinavian-style church.

ROUTE DIRECTIONS

① Cross stile at parking place and ascend cart-track. ② From gate/stile at end of plantation go straight ahead (FP Grassington) with broken wall on R. Pass to R of prominent rocky pinnacle and continue along level limestone terrace, crossing several ladder-stiles. ③ At 4-way guidepost go L (BW Conistone Moor 3¾) along vehicle track. ④ When it turns R take gate on L (FP Capplestone Gate). Follow path along RH side of field. Turn R (FP sign) at wall-corner, pass end of plantation and climb broad green path to o.s. column at Capplestone Gate. ⑤ Through gate/ladder-stile and turn L (FP Kettlewell). Follow sketchy path roughly parallel with wall on L until you reach a cross-fence (gate/stile). ⑥ A few yards beyond it take gate/ladder-stile on L. Descend steeply to path running about 50 yds from wall on L (For detour see notes on Langcliffe Pot). Path curves R to gap in broken wall. ⑦ Head R to descend RH side of very long field. Near its bottom end a tractor trail develops. Follow it through gate on R and downhill to rejoin outward route at point 2. Go R down cart-track.

SET IN THE HEART OF BEAUTIFUL WHARFEDALE, THIS SHORT WALK EMBODIES JUST ABOUT EVERY TYPICAL FEATURE OF DALES COUNTRY. HERE ARE WHITE LIMESTONE WALLS, PAVEMENTS AND GLEAMING SCARS, POTHOLES, DARK PLANTATIONS, ANCIENT PACKHORSE ROUTES, SOMBRE GRITSTONE MOORS AND REMAINS OF OLD MINING ACTIVITIES. HEIGHT IS GAINED EASILY, AND MOST OF THE WALKING IS ON DRY, CLOSE - CROPPED TURF. NOT RECOMMENDED IN ICY CONDITIONS.

35

ALTERNATIVE STARTS FROM CONISTONE

mast △

Scot Gate Lane

Conistone Dib

CONISTONE
(See Walk 3)

Two routes are available; both reach the circular walk at Point 3.
A : SCOT GATE LANE Walled track leaves the Kettlewell road (FP sign) 300 yards from village centre. A wearisome plod, best used for descent.
B : CONISTONE DIB Start up track from the village centre. Spectacular, but rough under-foot in places and ending with a rocky scramble. From ladder-stile at top turn left.

LANGCLIFFE POT
To visit this notorious pothole a short detour is necessary from point 6. On crossing

The limestone knoll of CONISTONE PIE is aptly named, for in distant views — particularly from the valley towards Kettlewell - it looks just like a pork pie. The small amount of extra effort needed to visit its neat little cairn is not wasted, this being a splendid vantage point for contemplating the beauty of Upper Wharfedale and Littondale.

the ladder-stile turn R to follow a faint track alongside the wall. About 50yds before reaching a crosswall turn down the slope to locate a shakehole with limestone blocks. Amongst these is a rather innocuous — looking hole, from which emanates the sound of flowing water. DO NOT VENTURE INTO IT, for it leads to a 90' pitch. The extensive system of underground passages is liable to flooding, and is regarded by cavers as one of the most difficult and dangerous in the country.

O.S. COLUMNS
OR, MORE CORRECTLY, ORDNANCE SURVEY TRIANGULATION PILLARS, DATE FROM THE RETRIANGULATION OF GREAT BRITAIN, BEGUN IN 1935 WHEN IT BECAME OBVIOUS THAT THE ORIGINAL SURVEY, STARTED AS LONG AGO AS 1791, WAS NO LONGER SUFFICIENTLY ACCURATE. ON TOP OF THE PILLAR ARE THREE BRASS GROOVES TO TAKE THE FEET OF THE SURVEYOR'S THEODOLITE, AND THREE LOOPS FOR TYING IT DOWN. THE PILLAR CONCEALS A TUBE IN WHICH THE THEODOLITE'S PLUMB LINE WILL HANG. ON ONE SIDE OF THE PILLAR IS A PLATE BEARING ATTACHMENT POINTS FOR A SPIRIT LEVEL, AND A BENCH MARK. THE HEIGHT OF THE STATION IS THE TIP OF THE ARROW. THE PILLARS ALSO MAKE JOLLY GOOD LEANING POSTS.

MAP O.S. Explorer OL2 Yorkshire Dales Southern and Western areas.

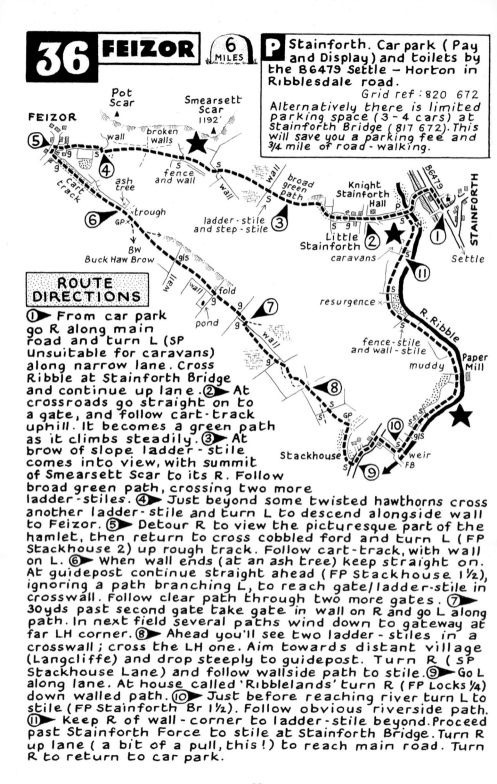

36 FEIZOR

6 MILES

P Stainforth. Car park (Pay and Display) and toilets by the B6479 Settle – Horton in Ribblesdale road.

Grid ref: 820 672

Alternatively there is limited parking space (3 – 4 cars) at Stainforth Bridge (817 672). This will save you a parking fee and 3/4 mile of road-walking.

Pot Scar

Smearsett Scar 1192'

FEIZOR

wall · broken walls

ash tree

fence and wall

trough GP×

BW Buck Haw Brow

ladder-stile and step-stile

Knight Stainforth Hall

broad green path

B6479

STAINFORTH

Little Stainforth caravans

Settle

resurgence ×

fence-stile and wall-stile

R. Ribble

muddy

Paper Mill

pond

fold

Stackhouse

GP

weir FB

ROUTE DIRECTIONS

① From car park go R along main road and turn L (SP Unsuitable for caravans) along narrow lane. Cross Ribble at Stainforth Bridge and continue up lane. ② At crossroads go straight on to a gate, and follow cart-track uphill. It becomes a green path as it climbs steadily. ③ At brow of slope ladder-stile comes into view, with summit of Smearsett Scar to its R. Follow broad green path, crossing two more ladder-stiles. ④ Just beyond some twisted hawthorns cross another ladder-stile and turn L to descend alongside wall to Feizor. ⑤ Detour R to view the picturesque part of the hamlet, then return to cross cobbled ford and turn L (FP Stackhouse 2) up rough track. Follow cart-track, with wall on L. ⑥ When wall ends (at an ash tree) keep straight on. At guidepost continue straight ahead (FP Stackhouse 1½), ignoring a path branching L, to reach gate/ladder-stile in crosswall. Follow clear path through two more gates. ⑦ 30yds past second gate take gate in wall on R and go L along path. In next field several paths wind down to gateway at far LH corner. ⑧ Ahead you'll see two ladder-stiles in a crosswall; cross the LH one. Aim towards distant village (Langcliffe) and drop steeply to guidepost. Turn R (SP Stackhouse Lane) and follow wallside path to stile. ⑨ Go L along lane. At house called 'Ribblelands' turn R (FP Locks ¼) down walled path. ⑩ Just before reaching river turn L to stile (FP Stainforth Br 1½). Follow obvious riverside path. ⑪ Keep R of wall-corner to ladder-stile beyond. Proceed past Stainforth Force to stile at Stainforth Bridge. Turn R up lane (a bit of a pull, this!) to reach main road. Turn R to return to car park.

82

A DELIGHTFUL EXCURSION INTO THE LONELY LIMESTONE UPLANDS WEST OF STAINFORTH, SKIRTING THE ROCKY HEIGHTS ABOVE THE PEACEFUL HAMLET OF FEIZOR. GOOD CLEAR PATHS GIVE EASY WALKING THROUGH TYPICAL LIMESTONE SCENERY OF SCARS, OUTCROPS AND GRASSY VALLEYS. A STROLL BESIDE A LOVELY STRETCH OF THE RIBBLE PROVIDES A NICELY CONTRASTING — THOUGH SOMETIMES MUDDY — FINISH.

36

KNIGHT STAINFORTH HALL is a square, solid, rather stern-looking structure. The present building is largely 17th C., but it is known that there was an earlier hall standing on the same site. Across the road is a popular caravan park.

FEIZOR
'Fayzer'

A remote hill-farming hamlet, with some traditional Dales cottages. On the tiny green stands a picturesque pump.

STACKHOUSE
is a pretty hamlet laid out around a maze of lanes and nestling in the lee of wooded limestone scars. There are several large houses, including the 17th C. Old Hall, once the home of James Carr, a local benefactor who founded Giggleswick School in the early years of the 16th C. In medieval times Stackhouse was a grange of Furness Abbey.

Ribblelands

Turn R here

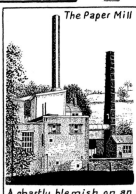

The Paper Mill

A ghastly blemish on an otherwise flawless riverscape

The **WEIR** was constructed to provide power for a water-mill. The 18th C. mill converted from corn to cotton in the early 1800s.

STAINFORTH FORCE & BRIDGE
are the highlights of a delightful stroll along the riverbank. Here the Ribble cascades over a series of wide limestone ledges into a big black pool. The graceful bridge was built in the 1670s by Samuel Watson, of nearby Knight Stainforth Hall. It is a typical packhorse bridge - very narrow and with low parapets designed so as not to obstruct the panniers slung over the horse's back.

MAP | O.S. Explorer OL 41 Forest of Bowland and Ribblesdale.

Cross bridge and take gated stile on L. (SP Mossdale Head 2m). Turn R to follow wall to river, then go L along waymarked riverside path. ② From ladder-stile rise to pass above trees to another ladder-stile. Bear ½ R (SP Mossdale Head) to come alongside a wall. ③ Cross ladder-stile and descend steeply through trees. Ford stream and go L to gate by barn. Keep straight on, then go R along farm road to A684. ④ For detour to Cotter Force (very easy, ¾ mile there and back, strongly recommended) go R along road, cross bridge and take path on L (FP Cotter Force 1¼ ML). Return to point 4 and continue along main road. ⑤ Take lane on R (Cotterdale only 1½) and immediately gate on L (Lady Ann (sic) Clifford's Highway R.U.P.P.). *Note: For easier alternative follow the tarmac road directly to point 7.* Follow wall on L. When it curves L keep straight on (marker posts) to climb alongside wall on L. ⑥ On reaching a stile in this wall don't use it, but turn R across the moor to a ladder-stile. Clear path descends — steeply in places — to reach road at a cattle-grid. ⑦ Go L along road to Cotterdale. ⑧ Near far end of hamlet take footbridge on R (FP Hardraw 3). Cross three fields via stiles. Keep along bottom of next field to a tiny fragment of wall then bear ½ L up to stile near trees. ⑨ Go R to stile by barn, then head for another prominent barn.

cont. below L

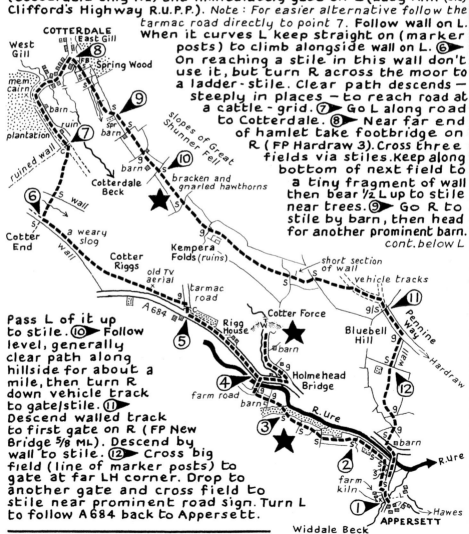

Pass L of it up to stile. ⑩ Follow level, generally clear path along hillside for about a mile, then turn R down vehicle track to gate/stile. ⑪ Descend walled track to first gate on R (FP New Bridge ⅝ ML). Descend by wall to stile. ⑫ Cross big field (line of marker posts) to gate at far LH corner. Drop to another gate and cross field to stile near prominent road sign. Turn L to follow A684 back to Appersett.

SHELTERED BY THE HIGH RIDGES OF LUNDS FELL AND GREAT SHUNNER FELL, COTTERDALE IS THE FIRST (OR LAST) OF WENSLEYDALE'S NUMEROUS SIDE-VALLEYS. IT IS A REMOTE AND TRANQUIL PLACE, ESPECIALLY BEAUTIFUL WHEN ITS MEADOWS ARE BEDECKED WITH SUMMER FLOWERS. GENERALLY AN EASY WALK, BUT WITH A RATHER TEDIOUS CLIMB UP THE RIDGE OF COTTER END (WHICH CAN BE AVOIDED). A WALKING-STICK IS HELPFUL ON THE STEEP DESCENT TO POINT 7. THE WALK IS NOT RECOMMENDED IN MIST.

Cotter Force

APPERSETT

A small village lying near the confluence of Widdale Beck and the River Ure, Appersett has no great pretensions to beauty. The name is of Norse origin; 'sett' is a corruption of 'sætr' - a farm, and the suffix occurs commonly in the Hawes area (Marsett, Countersett, Burtersett etc.).

COTTER FORCE is one of the lesser-known of Wensleydale's fine waterfalls, even though a path has been specially constructed to allow easy wheelchair access from the main road (where there's plenty of parking space). A stone bench invites you to sit and admire the scene. An idyllic picnic spot.

Lady Anne Clifford

Born at Skipton Castle on 30th January 1590, Lady Anne was the daughter of George Clifford, 3rd Earl of Cumberland. The family moved to London, and after the death of her father she had great difficulty in establishing her right to inherit his vast estate. She was, however, a stubborn and indomitable fighter, and after many years and many lawsuits she finally obtained possession of her properties. Returning north at the age of 60 she spent the next 26 years rebuilding churches and restoring the castles at Skipton, Pendragon, Brougham, Appleby and Brough to their former glory. She died on 22nd March 1676 and is buried beside her mother in Appleby church. The walk between points 5 and 6 follows part of the route she took when travelling to Pendragon - a road also used by drovers and packmen.

Look out for this little chap, the only Cotterdale resident ever seen by the author.

COTTERDALE

must be one of the quietest hamlets in the Dales. In several visits the author has never seen a living soul. Before crossing the footbridge at point 8 have a look at the houses at the far end of the hamlet. You will pass between cottages once inhabited by miners who were employed at the coal-pits a mile away up on the slopes of Great Shunner Fell. The last two buildings are Shepherd's Cottage, dated 1616, and the former Methodist chapel.

miners' cottages

GREAT SHUNNER FELL (2340') IS THE DALES' THIRD HIGHEST MOUNTAIN AFTER WHERNSIDE (2414') AND INGLEBOROUGH (2373').

MAP O.S. Explorer OL19 Howgill Fells

38 DALLOWGILL

5¾ MILES

P Dallowgill Moor. SEE LOCATION MAP. Parking place on minor road 3¾ miles WSW of Kirkby Malzeard. Park between farm road (sign Hawsett House) and wall. BE SURE NOT TO OBSTRUCT THE FARM ROAD.

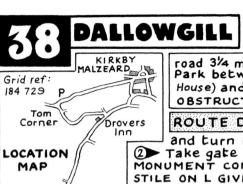

LOCATION MAP

Grid ref: 184 729

KIRKBY MALZEARD

Tom Corner

Drovers Inn

PATELEY BRIDGE

B6265 Ripon

B6165

ROUTE DIRECTIONS

① Go R up road and turn L (SP Dallowgill 1¼) at junction. ② Take gate on R in wall-angle (TO VISIT MONUMENT CONTINUE DOWN ROAD. LADDER-STILE ON L GIVES ACCESS. DETOUR BARELY ½ MILE THERE AND BACK). Follow track down, in last field bearing L to small gate at corner of barn. Straight on, passing L of house, and forward alongside wall on R to enter wood. ③ Follow path along top edge of wood. Take gate (wm) on L and go ½ R across field to stile. ④ Turn R down track. Cross footbridge and in 70yds turn L (sign Dallow) to another footbridge. Follow track rising R. ⑤ At far end of buildings turn L (wm) into farmyard. Keep R of all buildings and follow wall on L down to enter wood. When track forks keep L (small gate). Descend to footbridge and bear R up forest road. Go R along tarmac lane. ⑥ Fork L over cattle-grid and up farm road. When it turns L go straight on to gate. Go straight ahead to another gate, forward to pass L of wall-corner to another, then descend slightly R to gate. ⑦ Turn L along track (often muddy) which soon turns L to a gate. Turn *cont. below*

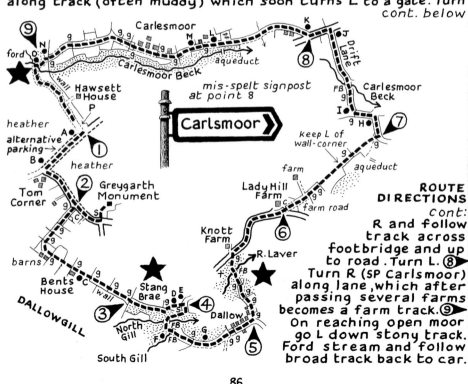

Carlesmoor

ford

aqueduct

Carlesmoor Beck

Drift Lane

⑧

Carlesmoor Beck

Hawsett House

heather

mis-spelt signpost at point 8

Carlsmoor ▶

keep L of wall-corner

alternative parking →

heather

farm

aqueduct

Tom Corner

② Greygarth Monument

Lady Hill Farm

farm road

⑥

Knott Farm

R. Laver

barns

Bents House

wall

Stang Brae

④

Dallow

⑤

③

DALLOWGILL

North Gill

South Gill

ROUTE DIRECTIONS *cont:* R and follow track across footbridge and up to road. Turn L. ⑧ Turn R (SP Carlsmoor) along lane, which after passing several farms becomes a farm track. ⑨ On reaching open moor go L down stony track. Ford stream and follow broad track back to car.

NESTLING IN A SECLUDED HOLLOW IN THE ROLLING MOORLAND EAST OF NIDDERDALE, ON THE FRINGE OF THE DALES, DALLOWGILL HAS A UNIQUE ATMOSPHERE OF PEACEFUL SERENITY. THE WALK HERE DESCRIBED IS A SHEER DELIGHT — A SEQUENCE OF BEAUTIFUL PLACES. THERE ARE ENCHANTING GREEN LANES, PURPLE MOORS, SPARKLING STREAMS AND LOVELY WOODLANDS, WITH SPLENDID VIEWS ALL ALONG THE WAY. THE WALK IS ESPECIALLY RECOMMENDED IN LATE MAY/EARLY JUNE, WHEN STANG BRAE WOOD IS CARPETED WITH BLUEBELLS.

CRACKPOTS MOSAIC TRAIL

The MOSAIC TRAIL at Dallowgill was created as part of a community project to celebrate the designation of NIDDERDALE as an AREA OF OUTSTANDING NATURAL BEAUTY. The mosaics were made during 1997 by THE CRACKPOTS from Kirkby Malzeard, under the expert supervision of Margaret Murphy from RURAL ARTS NORTH YORKSHIRE. The complete trail has 22 mosaics; this route takes in 15 of them, and their approximate locations are shown on the map:

- **A RED GROUSE** (made by Patrice Lyth)
- **B SHEEP** (Kirsty Hallett) • **C BENTS HOUSE** (Frances Lyth)
- **D BARN OWL** (Patrice Lyth) • **E RABBITS** (James Stewart)
- **F DEER** (Wahneta Thorne) • **G FUNGI** (Gwynneth Jackson)
- **H FLAG IRIS AND TADPOLES** (Hilda Roome and Nora Whipp)
- **I FRIESIAN COW** (Audrey Mackenzie) • **J GREATER SPOTTED WOODPECKER** (Sue Swales) • **K WILD ROSE** (Judy Schlehr)
- **L SIGHTING TOWER** (Naomi Lyth) • **M POTATO HOUSE** (Gwynneth Jackson) • **N ADDER** (Nora Whipp) • **O DRAGONFLY** (Margaret Crossfield)

THE GREYGARTH MONUMENT

WAS ORIGINALLY ERECTED BY THE LOCAL POPULACE IN 1897 TO COMMEMORATE QUEEN VICTORIA'S DIAMOND JUBILEE. THE PLAQUE RECORDS THAT THE EDIFICE WAS RESTORED BY LOCAL COUNCILS IN 1984. IT TAKES ONLY A FEW MINUTES TO CLIMB TO IT FROM THE ROAD, AND FROM THE METAL PLATFORM ATOP THE STRUCTURE THERE ARE EXTENSIVE VIEWS EASTWARD TOWARDS THE NORTH YORK MOORS.

Boulders just beyond point 7. The front boulder carries the Friesian Cow mosaic.

The famous American crooner **BING CROSBY** (1904-77) was fond of shooting on Dallowgill Moor.

The **RIVER LAVER** flows on to Ripon, where it joins the Skell and then the Ure.

MAP O.S. Explorer 26 Nidderdale

ROUTE DIRECTIONS

P Muker. Car park (pay and display - expensive) near bridge at E end of village. Grid ref: 911 978 Early birds will find roadside parking spaces in the village.

① From car park entrance take rough track (SP Occupation Road). ② At two adjacent gates on L take RH gate and follow thin, clear path with wall on L. ③ Go past farmhouse and on along farm road. Cross stone bridge and take metal gate on R. Climb gravel drive to house, take gated stile on R and bear L across field to stile. Climb alongside wall on L to reach slit-stile giving access to field with barn. ④ At this barn turn R to climb to stile in wall. Go L through gate then bear slightly R to stile at bend of tarmac road. Go R up road. ⑤ Just after passing small barn on L take stile on L (FP sign). Bear R down to field-corner, cross tiny stream and descend between stream and wall to gate/stile. Descend ½L to cross stream and go R up to gateway. ⑥ Follow wall on L, cross it through gap and stay with it to gate at top corner. Cross footbridge to obvious track slanting L up hillside. ⑦ When track bends R go straight ahead to fence-stile and path through trees, eventually dropping (FP sign) to stile in crosswall. ⑧ Cross bouldery hollow to thin path rising L to small gate. Forward to stile then continue along RH side of broken wall. When it ends keep straight on to come alongside wall on L and follow it past a farmhouse. ⑨ Descend tarmac road to Satron. ⑩ Cross main road and go down grassy ginnel. Take stile on L to flagged path. At barn take RH stile and head R. Pass R of farm buildings, bear L to stile and go L along riverside path. ⑪ Cross bridge and take stile on L (FP Muker). In second field keep R to small gate at far RH corner. Descend ½L to follow obvious riverside path for 1½ miles. ⑫ Cross big footbridge cont. below

⑫ Ramps Holme Bridge

Ramps Holme Farm

Meadowland - please walk in single file

Ivelet Bridge

MUKER

SATRON ⑩

car park ①

B6270

② barns

Rash

Rash Cottage

③

④

R. Swale

⑪

B6270

mem seat

Heugh

moorland road to Askrigg

FP

Oxnop Beck

tarmac

⑨

Gill Head (1847)

BEWARE OF HEADLESS DOGS

Rash Gill

⑤

small barn

ruin

⑥

FB

barn

⑦

old mines

⑧

ROUTE DIRECTIONS cont:
and follow wall on L to steps and stile (FP Muker). Follow flagged path through several meadows to village.

OF ALL THE WALKERS SETTING OFF FROM MUKER, THE VAST MAJORITY WILL BE POINTING THEIR BOOTS TOWARDS KISDON AND KELD, SO LET'S AVOID THE CROWDS BY HEADING DOWN - DALE THROUGH SOME OF THE LOVELIEST COUNTRYSIDE IN THE NATIONAL PARK. A BRIEF FORAY, ALONG LITTLE - USED PATHS, INTO THE HILLS ON THE SOUTH SIDE OF THE DALE IS FOLLOWED BY A DELIGHTFUL TWO - MILE RIVER - SIDE STROLL, MOSTLY ON SMOOTH, VELVETY TURF. THE WALK IS EASY, BUT MAY TAKE A LITTLE LONGER THAN YOU THINK, FOR THERE ARE NO FEWER THAN FIFTY GATES AND STILES TO NEGOTIATE, AND THE ROUTE IS SOMEWHAT COMPLEX IN THE VICINITIES OF RASH AND OXNOP BECK.

39

MUKER

Rash Cottage

Like many Swaledale villages, Muker (pro- nounced 'MOO-KER') owes its development to the lead-mining activities of the 18th and 19th centuries, and the grey stone miners' cottages huddle together in typical fashion. Tablets on the school wall commemorate two eminent former pupils, Richard and Cherry Kearton. The Kearton brothers, from nearby Thwaite, were pioneers in the development of the art of wildlife photography. The CHURCH OF ST. MARY was built in 1580 as a chapel-of- ease under Grinton, and was one of only a few churches to be built during the reign of Elizabeth I. Originally ling-thatched, the church was enlarged and given a new roof in 1761, and was much-restored in 1890. The LITERARY INSTITUTE (1868)

THE FARMERS ARMS

was built as a reading room. Today Muker is a popular centre for ramblers and tourists — a cheerful, self-sufficient little place with a cosy inn, shops and accommodation. All around are the barns and traditional flowery hay meadows for which Swaledale is renowned.

A highlight of the walk is the graceful IVELET BRIDGE (1695). At its north- east corner is the large, flat 'Coffin Stone,' said to be where coffins were rested during their portage along the 'Corpse Road' to Grinton Church. The bridge is reputed to be haunted by a headless dog, the sight of which will bring terrible ill-luck to its beholder. Alarming stuff! But at least it won't bite you, that's some consolation.

MAP OS Explorer OL 30 Yorkshire Dales Northern and Central areas.

40 BRIMHAM ROCKS

6½ MILES

P Dacre Banks. Layby by Holy Trinity Church. Grid ref: 197 622. Alternatively there's a large car park (pay and display) at Brimham Rocks. Grid ref: 208 645

ROUTE DIRECTIONS

① ▶ Walk away from Dacre Banks, cross main road and up Hartwith Bank. ② ▶ Turn L (FP Old Spring Wood) and follow clear, level woodland path. Cross stile and continue along edge of wood. ③ ▶ Take gate on L near shed to enter enclosed track. Pass L of farm and on along track. ④ ▶ 50yds from end of wood turn R up thin path. Keep near edge of wood to stile, then straight across field to gate/stile. Go L along road. ⑤ ▶ Take gate (FP sign) near small ruin. Cross field to stile near far LH corner. Follow line of former hedge across next field to stile. Turn R and follow broad track which climbs to meet tarmac road ⑥ ▶ Go L up road and fork L up road through car park. ⑦ ▶ Go L up path which starts at info. board. Use the many paths to explore the rocks and eventually arrive at Brimham House. ⑧ ▶ Go up round LH end of buildings to broad path passing the 'Dancing Bear' rock. When path forks keep L. Path heads towards heather moorland, but don't go on to it — turn L to descend clear path. ⑨ ▶ Go sharp L down farm road. When it turns R towards farm go straight on through gate. Take fence-stile on R and drop to a track L of house (FP sign). ⑩ ▶ When track swings R go straight on to ladder-stile. Descend to go L between walls to stile. Descend RH edge of field. Pass through two gates then turn L to cross fields (no path — don't lose any height) to fence-stile into wood. ⑪ ▶ Straight on along thin path, through unusual gate with integral stile and turn R to pass in front of house. Bear L down walled track. ⑫ ▶ In a few yards go L along woodland path. Near some brick buildings turn sharp R, cross footbridge and follow path downstream. ⑬ ▶ Go L along road for ⅓ mile. Turn R (FP sign) along farm road. ⑭ ▶ Go through farmyard. On reaching a pond (on your L) turn R along farm road (modern barns on your L). ⑮ ▶ Cross stile on L. Turn R to descend through gap in trees to stile at LH end of high wall. Straight on to join drive then L along main road.

farm road
heather
o.s. col.
Brimham House
info., shop, refreshments, toilets
BRIMHAM ROCKS
car park
farm road
holly
muddy
Fell Beck
FB
pond
tedious trudge
fence
High Wood
ruin
Smelthouses
Braisty Woods Farm
barns
bracken
THE NATIONAL TRUST
BRIMHAM ROCKS
Woolwich Farm
pond
barns
shed
Pateley Bridge
Birch Wood
Old Spring Wood
B 6165
R. Nidd
Meth. church
pond
layby
Summerbridge
DACRE BANKS
Ripley B6165
cricket ground

40

BRIMHAM ROCKS ARE ONE OF THE DALES' MAJOR TOURIST ATTRACTIONS, AND UNDERSTANDABLY SO, FOR THESE IMMENSE AND GROTESQUELY ERODED BLOCKS OF GRITSTONE CONSTITUTE A UNIQUE PIECE OF BRITISH SCENERY. THE PANORAMIC VIEWS AND THE MAGNIFICENT WOODLAND PATHS MAKE THIS A WALK OF TRULY OUTSTANDING BEAUTY AND INTEREST. ON A SUNNY AUTUMN DAY THE COLOURS ARE QUITE SENSATIONAL. THE ROUTE IS FAIRLY COMPLEX – PARTICULARLY BETWEEN POINTS 8 AND 12 – SO PAY CLOSE ATTENTION TO THE MAP AND ROUTE DIRECTIONS.

By using the short section of road marked ✣ on the map you have the option of TWO SEPARATE SHORT WALKS :–
1. Dacre Banks – Woolwich Farm – Braisty Woods – Dacre Banks (2¾ miles).
2. (Park at Brimham Rocks) Rocks – Smelthouses – High Wood – Rocks (3¾ miles).

HOLY TRINITY CHURCH, DACRE BANKS, from where the walk begins, was built in 1837 at a time when there was great poverty in the area due to the decline of the local flax-spinning industry. The tower was originally topped by a wooden spire, which was removed in July 1918 having become thoroughly worm-eaten and decayed. A fire on 21 October 1991 caused severe damage. Repairs to the organ alone cost £40,000, and the total restoration bill was £120,000. Externally the church has a somewhat austere appearance, but the interior has a welcoming atmosphere and is obviously lovingly cared-for.

BRIMHAM'S TWO MOST FAMOUS ROCKS
are encountered between points 8 and 9

The Dancing Bear   The Idol

The rocks stand at nearly 1,000' on the edge of the moor above a windswept escarpment. The groups and individual blocks form bizarre shapes, and most have had names bestowed upon them. Some, like 'The Dancing Bear,' are easily recognised, while others require an imagination a great deal more fanciful than the author's. 'The Idol' is a 180 ton boulder perched on a tiny pedestal only 18" thick. Though folklore would have us believe that the rocks were fashioned by Druids, geologists will tell us that they have been 300 million years in the making. Brimham House, built in 1792 as a shooting lodge, is now an excellent Information Centre. The National Trust acquired the property in 1970 and has considerably improved visitor facilities.

SMELTHOUSES is so named because Fountains Abbey had a lead smelting mill here. The earliest flax mill in Nidderdale was established here in 1798. It was gutted by fire in 1890.

★

SUMMERBRIDGE dates mostly from the 19th C., when there were 5 mills here. It's quite a sizeable village, with a few shops, a large Methodist church, a pub and – best of all – a great little 'chippy'.

THE CHIPPY AT SUMMERBRIDGE

MAP	O.S. Explorer 26 Nidderdale.

41 BORDLEY TOWN

7½ MILES

P Malham Moor Lane. Just N of Threshfield on the B6160 is a lane, signposted 'Skirethorns'. Motor along this lane (which turns sharp R at Skirethorns) for nearly 2 miles, until you see 2 signposts (BW Boss Moor and BW Kilnsey) opposite each other. Park here on the grass verge.

Grid ref : 960 650

ROUTE DIRECTIONS

① ► Walk back down the lane for about a mile. ② ► Turn R through ornamental gates of Wood Nook (FP Bordley). Pass R of house and go straight on along LH path to corner-stile. ③ ► Cross stream and follow it uphill (marker-posts). When stream veers L keep straight on along clear path. Pass L of derelict farmhouse to follow wall on L to gate in fence, then straight ahead with wall on R. ④ ► Turn R (FP sign). Go down between barns and up to gated stile on L. Climb with wall on L to step-stile and keep L of barn to follow clear path passing between kiln (R) and rocky hollow (L). ⑤ ► When main path veers R fork L (FP sign) and follow wall on L. Descend steeply, cross stile and climb with wall on L. ⑥ ► Turn R up tarmac farm road. ⑦ ► When tarmac road turns R go straight ahead (BW Kilnsey 2½) along level path with wall on R. ⑧ ► Turn R through gate (BW Kilnsey 2) and follow walled green lane for 1½ miles. ⑨ ► Pass through a gate and immediately turn sharp R (FP sign). Through gated sheep pens and forward along track, which soon acquires a fence on its R. When track swings L it fragments into several paths. Take your pick — they all join up to climb through a shallow but obvious valley (blue-topped marker-posts). ⑩ From gate in crosswall keep straight on. Clear path (with marker-posts) eventually descends to a gate at our starting-point.

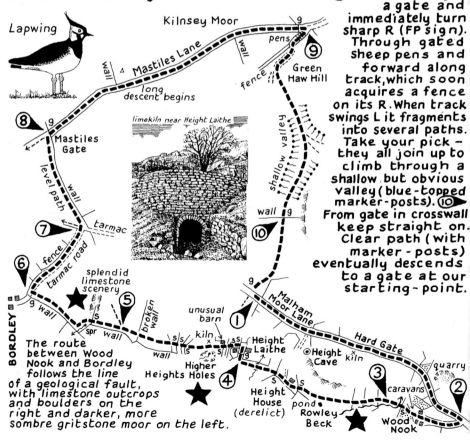

Lapwing

Kilnsey Moor

Mastiles Lane

wall

long descent begins

△

pens

wall

fence

Green Haw Hill

⑨

shallow valley

limekiln near Height Laithe

⑧ ◄ 9

Mastiles Gate

level path

wall

fence

⑦ ► tarmac

⑥ ◄

tarmac road

fence

splendid limestone scenery

⑤ ►

broken wall

spr wall

wall 9

BORDLEY

9 wall

s

s

wall 9

⑩ ◄

unusual barn

kiln

s/s

s/s

① 9

s/s

Height Laithe

Malham Moor Lane

Hard Gate

Height Cave

kiln

③

quarry

caravans

②

s/s

Wood Nook

Higher Heights Holes

④

Height House (derelict)

pond

Rowley Beck

The route between Wood Nook and Bordley follows the line of a geological fault, with limestone outcrops and boulders on the right and darker, more sombre gritstone moor on the left.

SET IN THE PEACEFUL, ROLLING HILLS BETWEEN GRASSINGTON AND MALHAM, THIS TYPICAL DALES WALK IS ONE OF MARKED CONTRASTS. THE SOUTHERN SECTION IS EXQUISITELY BEAUTIFUL, WHILST TO THE NORTH THE ROUTE TRAVERSES BARE AND WINDSWEPT UPLANDS. ALTHOUGH THERE ARE NO REALLY STEEP GRADIENTS, THE WALK IS UNDULATING AND MODERATELY STRENUOUS. SHOULD THE WEATHER TURN NASTY, YOU MAY MAKE A QUICK RETURN TO THE CAR BY REMAINING ON THE FARM ROAD AT POINT 7, THEREBY OMITTING THE MASTILES SECTION AND REDUCING THE WALK TO 4¾ MILES.

41

HEIGHT CAVE ☆

is prominently in view in a small cliff on the R at the start of the walk. What appears to be two separate caves is actually a common entrance split by a rock pillar. The cave has a number of alternative names (Heights Cave, Skythorns Cave, Calf Hole, Elland Cave). It is on private land, and a 'KEEP OUT' sign on a padlocked gate suggests that visitors are not welcome. Various Iron - and Bronze - age tools and weapons have been found here, some of which are on display at the Craven Museum in Skipton.

HIGHER HEIGHTS HOLES

are three potholes at the E. end of a large hollow. The LH hole (illustrated R) swallows a small stream.

LIMEKILNS

The unusual barn

In the mid - 18th C. Dales farmers began to construct intake walls to enclose land on the edges of the moors. The new fields needed to be burned, drained and limed, and kilns were built to produce the huge amounts of lime required. The dry-stone masonry of the kiln had a funnel-shaped lining of brick or sandstone, and beneath the narrow neck at its base was the grate for collecting lime and ash. A mixture of coal and limestone was fed into the top of the kiln and was fired by burning wood at the base. Once fired the kiln would usually be kept going for 2 - 3 days, by which time it would have produced some 30-40 tons of lime — enough to treat about 6 - 8 acres of land. Many farms had their own kilns, and some of the larger ones produced lime on a commercial basis. Limekilns had gone out of use by about 1860, but hundreds survive throughout the Dales. The one seen on this walk is a typical example.

BORDLEY

MAY BE VISITED BY MAKING A SHORT DETOUR FROM POINT 6, BUT THERE'S NOT MUCH TO SEE, FOR THIS IS ABOUT AS SMALL AS A HAMLET GETS — JUST 2 FARMS. IN THE MIDDLE AGES, HOWEVER, IT WAS LARGE ENOUGH TO HAVE THE STATUS OF A 'TOWNSHIP', AND IS STILL SOMETIMES REFERRED TO AS 'BORDLEY TOWN' BY LOCAL PEOPLE. IT WAS A GRANGE OF FOUNTAINS ABBEY.

MASTILES LANE

is a classic 'green road'- the most famous of all the many old drovers' roads in the Dales. In those days the lane would be unwalled, the route being way-marked by stone crosses.

Sign at Mastiles Gate

MAP O.S. Explorer OL2 Yorkshire Dales Southern and Western areas.

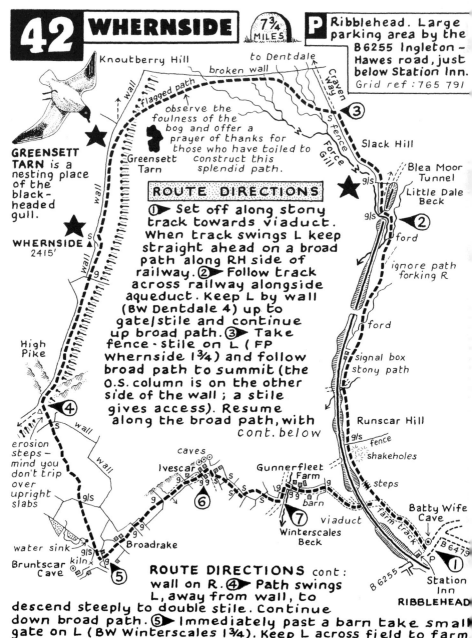

P Ribblehead. Large parking area by the B6255 Ingleton–Hawes road, just below Station Inn. Grid ref: 765 791

Knoutberry Hill

to Dentdale

broken wall

flagged path

wall

Craven Way

③

Slack Hill

S fence

Force Gill

observe the foulness of the bog and offer a prayer of thanks for those who have toiled to construct this splendid path.

Greensett Tarn

GREENSETT TARN is a nesting place of the black-headed gull.

Blea Moor Tunnel

Little Dale Beck

gls

②

ford

ignore path forking R

WHERNSIDE ▲ 2415'

wall

ford

signal box

stony path

Runscar Hill

gls fence

shakeholes

High Pike

④

erosion steps – mind you don't trip over upright slabs

wall

wall

gls

caves

Ivescar

⑥

Gunnerfleet Farm

barn

⑦

viaduct

Winterscales Beck

steps

farm track

Batty Wife Cave

B6479

water sink

Broadrake

gls

Bruntscar Cave

kiln

⑤

①

Station Inn

RIBBLEHEAD

B6255

ROUTE DIRECTIONS

①➤ Set off along stony track towards viaduct. When track swings L keep straight ahead on a broad path along RH side of railway. ②➤ Follow track across railway alongside aqueduct. Keep L by wall (BW Dentdale 4) up to gate/stile and continue up broad path. ③➤ Take fence-stile on L (FP Whernside 1¾) and follow broad path to summit (the O.S. column is on the other side of the wall; a stile gives access). Resume along the broad path, with *cont. below*

ROUTE DIRECTIONS cont: wall on R. ④➤ Path swings L, away from wall, to descend steeply to double stile. Continue down broad path. ⑤➤ Immediately past a barn take small gate on L (BW Winterscales 1¾). Keep L across field to farm Pass R of all buildings and go straight on through a series of small gates, eventually joining a cart-track to Ivescar Farm. ⑥➤ Enter farmyard and turn R at junction of farm roads. Immediately past barn take stile on L. Go R across field to stile (wm). Follow wall over hill and down to gated stile at wall-corner. Head for viaduct to locate next stile, then go forward with wall on L. ⑦➤ Go L along farm road. Turn R over farm bridge and follow farm road under viaduct and back to car.

STRENUOUS, WITH A 2¼-MILE-LONG CLIMB OF 1,300' FROM THE AQUEDUCT TO THE SUMMIT. THE WALK IS ALMOST ENTIRELY ON CLEAR TRACKS AND PATHS, AND IS PERFECTLY SAFE - THOUGH PERHAPS A WASTE OF ENERGY - IN MIST, BUT SHOULD NOT BE ATTEMPTED IN SEVERE WINTRY CONDITIONS. AFTER HEAVY OR PROLONGED RAIN THE FORDING OF LITTLE DALE BECK MAY PROVE DIFFICULT (TIP - POP A COUPLE OF PLASTIC BIN-LINERS INTO YOUR RUCKSACK). THE DESCENT FROM POINT 4 IS STEEP AND ROUGH, AND **NEEDS CARE.** THE VIEWS ARE QUITE BREATHTAKING.

42

THE SETTLE-CARLISLE RAILWAY
A MARVEL OF VICTORIAN ENGINEERING

1875-1991

Detail from the memorial plaque, Ribblehead viaduct.

The story of the building of this famous railway is one of enthusiasm, determination and, above all, incredible toil and hardship during some of the worst winters of the 19thC. The ambitious project was begun in November 1869, when the first sod was cut near Settle Junction. After the construction of 72 miles of track, 325 bridges, 21 viaducts, 14 tunnels and 103 culverts, the line was declared open on 2 August 1875. The best-known and most stunning feature of the whole colossal enterprise is the mighty, 24-arch RIBBLEHEAD VIADUCT (properly called Batty Moss Viaduct), the first stone of which was laid on 12 October 1870. The foundations had to be sunk 25' through peat and clay to solid rock, and there were countless other problems - the hardness of the stone, flooding of the quarries, the sogginess of the moor, blizzards, and winds so violent that the brickies were unable to work for fear of being blown off the scaffolding. The quarter-mile-long, 104' high viaduct was completed in October 1874. Following recent restoration work a most interesting commemorative stone was placed below the 14th arch. Some 300 miners, bricklayers and labourers were employed in building BLEA MOOR TUNNEL. Progressing at the rate of about 16 yards a week they took 5 years to finish the job. The tunnel is 2629 yards long and at one point is 500' below the surface of the moor. One of the 3 ventilation shafts is 360' deep. The thousands of navvies engaged on this work lived in 'shanty towns', the names of which can be seen on the commemorative stone.

WHERNSIDE

The summit

ALTHOUGH THE HIGHEST OF THE FAMOUS 'THREE PEAKS', WHERNSIDE IS NOT BLESSED WITH SUCH DRAMATIC PROFILES AS ARE INGLEBOROUGH AND PENYGHENT. IN FACT IT HAS TO BE CONCEDED THAT FROM MOST ANGLES IT LOOKS PRETTY BORING. THE SUMMIT, TOO, IS DREARY, BUT THE WALK TO IT AND FROM IT, ALONG THE RIM OF THE PLUNGING ESCARPMENT, IS SHEER BLISS. THE RETROSPECTIVE VIEW IS OF THE HOWGILLS AND THE EXQUISITE DENTDALE BEYOND WHERNSIDE TARNS. AWAY TO THE LEFT THE DALES FELLS STRETCH SEEMINGLY TO INFINITY, WHILST NEARBY AND STRAIGHT AHEAD LOOMS THE MAJESTIC INGLEBOROUGH.

MAP O.S. Explorer OL 2 Yorkshire Dales Southern and Western areas.

43 LOWER COVERDALE

6¾ MILES

P Middleham. Park in the Market Square.
Grid ref: 127 877

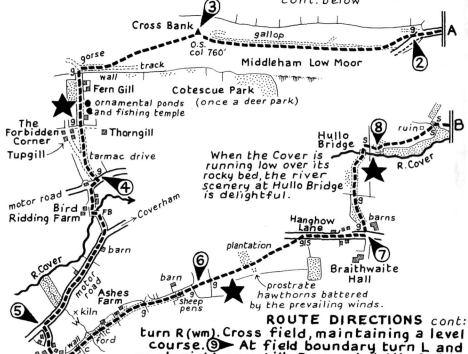

ROUTE DIRECTIONS

① Leave Market Square by the Coverdale road at its top LH corner. ② Take fence-gate on R (BW sign). Bear L to a horse-gallop and follow it up to O.S. column. ③ Bear ½L, aiming towards lower end of Penhill. Join vehicle track with wall on your L. Turn L through stone gateway to walled track. Keep straight on. Track eventually becomes a tarmac drive. ④ Turn R along road. In 60 yds go L along farm road. DON'T enter farmyard. Keep L by cottage down narrow path to cross footbridge and rise to road. Follow it forward for ½ mile. ⑤ Turn L (SP Caldbergh Only). Climb through hamlet to gate and follow farm track, which eventually becomes a green path alongside wall on L. ⑥ When wall turns away L keep straight on. Pass R of plantation then bear slightly L and descend big field to gate/stile at its far corner. Go R along lane. ⑦ Take gate on L (BW Hullo Bridge ⅓) and follow old cart-track down to river. Cross bridge and take stile (wm) on R. ⑧ Climb clear path through trees and cross field to stile (wm). Pass through narrow stand of Scots pines and *cont. below*

MIDDLEHAM

① Castle

A

William's Hill (site of former castle)

wall

gis

barn

⑨

B

③ Cross Bank

gallop

gorse

O.S. col 760'

track

Middleham Low Moor

② A

wall

Fern Gill

Cotescue Park *(once a deer park)*

ornamental ponds and fishing temple

The Forbidden Corner

Tupgill

Thorngill

tarmac drive

⑧ ruin s s B

Hullo Bridge s

R. Cover

When the Cover is running low over its rocky bed, the river scenery at Hullo Bridge is delightful.

motor road

Bird Ridding Farm

FB

Coverham

④

Hanghow Lane

gis

barns

⑦

R. Cover

plantation

Braithwaite Hall

⑥

barn

barn

prostrate hawthorns battered by the prevailing winds.

sheep pens

R. Cover

motor road

Ashes Farm

× kiln

w

c

c ford

⑤

wall

CALDBERGH

ROUTE DIRECTIONS *cont:*
turn R (wm). Cross field, maintaining a level course. ⑨ At field boundary turn L and go straight on uphill. From gate/stile follow wall on L to join lane passing R of castle.

THE ANCIENT TOWN OF MIDDLEHAM, FAMOUS FOR ITS CASTLE AND ITS RACEHORSES, IS THE STARTING POINT FOR THIS DELIGHTFUL RAMBLE. FROM THE LOW MOOR, WHERE THE VELVETY TURF IS A JOY TO TREAD, THERE ARE GLORIOUS VIEWS OF COVERDALE, PENHILL AND WENSLEYDALE. WITH ITS GENTLE GRADIENTS THIS IS AN IDEAL WALK FOR A WARM SUMMER'S DAY. KEEP A SHARP LOOK-OUT FOR THE CROCODILE.

43

Middleham Church

MIDDLEHAM
☆

Colourful three-storeyed Georgian houses and inns give this little town a most elegant air. The Swine Cross in the upper market place commemorates the 1479 ratification of the Market Charter given to the town a century earlier. Middleham is renowned for its castle and its racing stables. Racehorses have been trained here for over two centuries (the first recognised trainer was Isaac Cape (1720-90) who lived at Tupgill). Middleham Low Moor, to the west of the town, provides excellent training gallops.

THE SPLENDID **CHURCH OF ST. MARY AND ST. ALKELDA** SHOULD NOT BE MISSED. THE PRESENT BUILDING DATES MOSTLY FROM THE 13TH AND 14TH CENTURIES. THE SITE IS THOUGHT TO BE THE FINAL RESTING PLACE OF ALKELDA, A 9TH C. PRINCESS WHO WAS STRANGLED WITH HER OWN HAIR BY DANISH WOMEN FOR REFUSING TO RENOUNCE HER CHRISTIAN FAITH.

THE NORMAN CASTLE, with its massive 12th C.

keep - one of the largest in England — dominates the little town. The castle was started c 1170, and in the 14th C. became the stronghold of the powerful Neville family. It was at the height of power in the 15th C. when in the hands of Richard Neville, Earl of Warwick, aka Warwick the Kingmaker. On his death in 1471 the castle went to the crown, and Edward IV gave it to his brother Richard (later III). The walls of the keep stand almost to their original height, and other notable remains are the gatehouse, chapel and banqueting hall. To the SW is the site of an early Norman wooden castle.

Richard III
1452-1485

The Fishing Temple at Tupgill.

The Forbidden Corner

is a delightful four-acre walled garden filled with quirky features to explore - a great day out for all the family, but prebooking is essential.

CALDBERGH *is thought to be the birthplace of Miles Coverdale (see Walk 50).*

BRAITHWAITE HALL IS A SPLENDID 17TH C. HOUSE NOW IN THE CARE OF THE NATIONAL TRUST. IT CAN BE VISITED BY PRIOR APPOINTMENT.

MAP | O.S. Explorer OL 30 Yorkshire Dales Northern and Central areas.

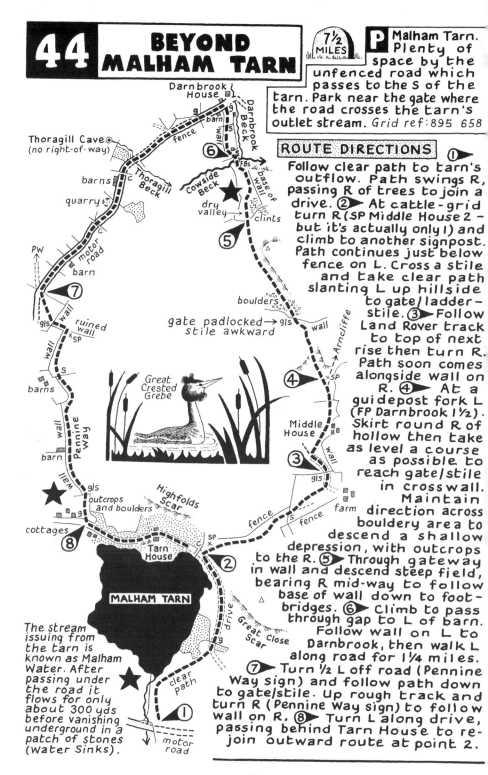

44 BEYOND MALHAM TARN

7½ MILES

P Malham Tarn. Plenty of space by the unfenced road which passes to the S of the tarn. Park near the gate where the road crosses the tarn's outlet stream. *Grid ref: 895 658*

ROUTE DIRECTIONS

①➤ Follow clear path to tarn's outflow. Path swings R, passing R of trees to join a drive. ②➤ At cattle-grid turn R (SP Middle House 2 – but it's actually only 1) and climb to another signpost. Path continues just below fence on L. Cross a stile and take clear path slanting L up hillside to gate/ladder-stile. ③➤ Follow Land Rover track to top of next rise then turn R. Path soon comes alongside wall on R. ④➤ At a guidepost fork L (FP Darnbrook 1½). Skirt round R of hollow then take as level a course as possible to reach gate/stile in crosswall. Maintain direction across bouldery area to descend a shallow depression, with outcrops to the R. ⑤➤ Through gateway in wall and descend steep field, bearing R mid-way to follow base of wall down to foot-bridges. ⑥➤ Climb to pass through gap to L of barn. Follow wall on L to Darnbrook, then walk L along road for 1¼ miles. ⑦➤ Turn ½ L off road (Pennine Way sign) and follow path down to gate/stile. Up rough track and turn R (Pennine Way sign) to follow wall on R. ⑧➤ Turn L along drive, passing behind Tarn House to re-join outward route at point 2.

Darnbrook House

Darnbrook Beck

Thoragill Cave (no right-of-way)

Thoragill Beck

barns

quarry

Cowside Beck

dry valley

clints

base of wall

FBs

⑥

⑤

PW

motor road

barn

⑦

ruined wall

gls

xSP

wall

S

barns

wall

Pennine Way

barn

boulders

gate padlocked→
stile awkward

gls

wall

Arncliffe

SP

④

Middle House

wall

③

gls

Great Crested Grebe

gls

outcrops and boulders

cottages

⑧

Highfolds Scar

Tarn House

SP

②

fence

S

fence

farm

MALHAM TARN

drive

Great Close Scar

The stream issuing from the tarn is known as Malham Water. After passing under the road it flows for only about 300 yds before vanishing underground in a patch of stones (Water Sinks).

clear path

①

motor road

98

44

LEAVE THE MADDING CROWD BEHIND IN THE SPECTACULAR TRIANGLE OF COUNTRY WHICH HAS THE COVE AND GORDALE SCAR AS ITS BASE, AND VENTURE BEYOND MALHAM TARN AT ITS APEX INTO THE AREA KNOWN AS MALHAM MOOR. THE SCENERY MAY BE TAME BY COMPARISON WITH THE 'TRIANGLE', BUT THIS IS FINE WALKING TERRAIN — AND YOU WON'T HAVE TO QUEUE TO CROSS THE STILES!

IN MIST THE SECTION ACROSS THE MOOR (POINTS 4 - 5) MAY REQUIRE THE USE OF A COMPASS.

crayfish

THE NATIONAL TRUST
MALHAM TARN ESTATE

MALHAM TARN

is not something you would expect to see in this limestone country, for limestone, being porous, does not hold surface water. Malham Tarn, however, lies on an intrusive bed of Silurian slate, which is impervious, and its waters are contained by moraines of glacial debris. It is a beautiful lake in a quite superb setting, and is an immensely popular venue for walkers, picnickers and bird-watchers. The tarn is a home and sanctuary for a variety of waders and waterfowl. Look out especially for the great crested grebe, one of our loveliest water birds. The lime-rich water of the

the outflow

tarn is an ideal habitat for the crayfish, and also contains a species of flightless caddis-fly that, so far as is known, occurs nowhere else in Britain.

Malham Tarn lies at 1230' above sea-level and has a surface area of 153 acres, but is shallow, being nowhere more than 14' deep. Long years ago it belonged to Fountains Abbey; now it is part of the National Trust's Malham Tarn Estate, a National Nature Reserve and SSSI (site of Special Scientific Interest).

TARN HOUSE WAS BUILT c 1780 AS A SHOOTING LODGE FOR LORD LISTER, AND IN 1852 BECAME THE COUNTRY SEAT OF THE MORRISON FAMILY. SINCE 1948 IT HAS BEEN A FIELD STUDIES CENTRE. CHARLES KINGSLEY (1819-75) FOUND INSPIRATION HERE TO WRITE 'THE WATER BABIES' (PUBLISHED 1863).

TWO ANCIENT HOUSES **MIDDLE HOUSE** was built in the late 16th C on the site of a much older building which belonged to Fountains Abbey. The house was rebuilt in the 1620s, and the porch was added in the late 17th C. **DARNBROOK HOUSE**, still a working farm, has some 600 years of history, though the present building mostly dates from the 17th C. Beside the farmhouse wall is a pothole — Robinson's Pot — which leads to an extensive cave system.

Middle House

Darnbrook House

MAP O.S. Explorer OL 2 Yorkshire Dales Southern and Western areas.

45 BUCKDEN PIKE

7½ MILES

P Buckden. Large car park (pay and display) at N end of village. *Grid ref: 943 774*

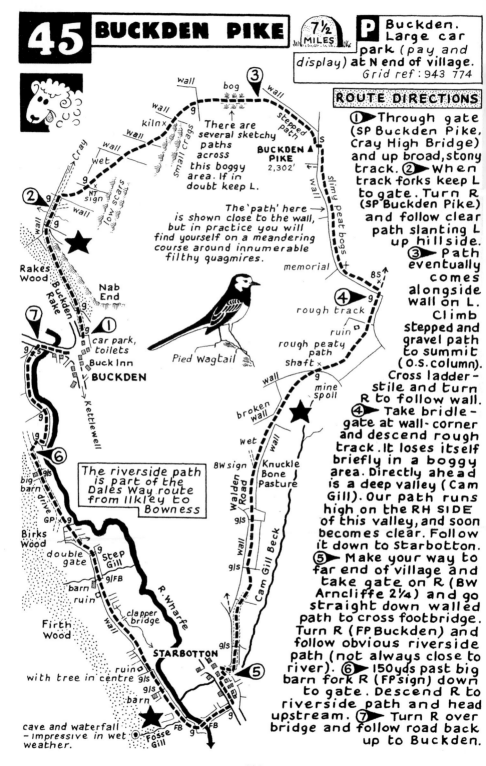

wall

bog

③

wall

wall

stepped path

kiln

small crags

BUCKDEN PIKE 2,302'

There are several sketchy paths across this boggy area. If in doubt keep L.

NT sign

The 'path' here is shown close to the wall, but in practice you will find yourself on a meandering course around innumerable filthy quagmires.

Cray

wet

low scars

②

wall

memorial

sliny peat bogs

Rakes Wood

Nab End

④

rough track

Buckden Rake

⑦

①

car park, toilets

ruin

rough peaty path

Buck Inn

BUCKDEN

Pied Wagtail

shaft

mine spoil

wall

Kettlewell

broken wall

⑥

The riverside path is part of the Dales Way route from Ilkley to Bowness

wet

BW sign

Knuckle Bone Pasture

big barn

drive

GP

Birks Wood

Walden Road

double gate

Step Gill

barn ruin

clapper bridge

R. Wharfe

Cam Gill Beck

Firth Wood

STARBOTTON

with tree in centre

ruin

barn

⑤

cave and waterfall – impressive in wet weather.

Fosse Gill

ROUTE DIRECTIONS

① Through gate (SP Buckden Pike, Cray High Bridge) and up broad, stony track. ② When track forks keep L to gate. Turn R (SP Buckden Pike) and follow clear path slanting L up hillside. ③ Path eventually comes alongside wall on L. Climb stepped and gravel path to summit (O.S. column). Cross ladder-stile and turn R to follow wall. ④ Take bridle-gate at wall-corner and descend rough track. It loses itself briefly in a boggy area. Directly ahead is a deep valley (Cam Gill). Our path runs high on the RH SIDE of this valley, and soon becomes clear. Follow it down to Starbotton. ⑤ Make your way to far end of village and take gate on R (BW Arncliffe 2¼) and go straight down walled path to cross footbridge. Turn R (FP Buckden) and follow obvious riverside path (not always close to river). ⑥ 150yds past big barn fork R (FP sign) down to gate. Descend R to riverside path and head upstream. ⑦ Turn R over bridge and follow road back up to Buckden.

A STRENUOUS BUT VERY POPULAR WALK OFFERING A WIDE VARIETY OF TERRAIN AND SCENERY. AFTER A CLIMB OF JUST OVER 1,500' TO THE SUMMIT, THERE ARE SUPERB VIEWS OF UPPER WHARFEDALE AS A LONG DESCENT IS MADE, DOWN AN ANCIENT PACKHORSE TRACK, TO THE LITTLE VILLAGE OF STARBOTTON. THE EASY RIVERSIDE RETURN FOLLOWS AN ATTRACTIVE SECTION OF THE MUCH-TRODDEN DALES WAY. THE ¾ MILE STRETCH BETWEEN THE SUMMIT AND POINT 4 IS JUICY, TO PUT IT MILDLY, AND WILL BE ENJOYED ONLY BY DEDICATED BOG-TROTTERS. IF CAUGHT IN MIST IT WOULD BE ADVISABLE TO RETRACE STEPS FROM THE SUMMIT.

45

BUCKDEN

was, in medieval times, the HQ of the foresters of Langstrothdale Chase. The highly popular Buck Inn, with a deer on its sign, reveals the origin of the village's name. Buckden stands at the last 'turning-point' of Upper Wharfedale, where a road leads off W to Hawes whilst the main road heads N through Cray and over Kidstones Pass to Bishopdale.

LONE ✝ SURVIVOR....

On 31 January 1942 an RAF Wellington bomber, crewed by six Polish airmen, crashed on Buckden Pike in a blizzard. Jozef Fusniak, the rear gunner — badly injured but the sole survivor — crawled from the wreckage to find, nearby, the footprints of a fox in the snow. He followed the tracks downhill, and eventually they led him to a farm and safety. In 1973 Mr. Fusniak returned to erect a cross at the scene of the crash, in thanksgiving for his escape and in memory of the five men who died. Below the inscription is a bronze fox's head, and fragments of the wreckage are set into the concrete base.

BUCKDEN RAKE

follows the line of a Roman road linking Olicana (Ilkley) and Virosidum (Bainbridge).

Dales walker c 80 AD

BUCKDEN PIKE

is not really a pike (*) at all, for its top is flat and extensive. The unattractive summit has an untidy cairn, a ladder-stile and an O.S. column which in wet weather stands in the middle of a black, slimy pool.
* pike — the peaked top of a hill.

The small village of **STARBOTTON** is what remains of a much larger lead-mining community. Its focal point is the excellent Fox and Hounds (1834) where you can enjoy Timothy Taylor's ale, the finest beer in Yorkshire (in the author's humble opinion).

WALDEN ROAD

is an old packhorse route from Wharfedale to Wensleydale. The small ruin near the top is thought to have been a shelter for packhorsemen and drovers.

boundary stone, point 4

Fox and Hounds Inn, Starbotton.

MAP O.S. Explorer OL 30 Yorkshire Dales Northern and Central areas.

46 BOOZE 4¾ MILES

Booze Moor ④
gully
butt (N°9) ×
bell pits
cairn on top of bell pit
This cairn commands a superb view of Upper Arkengarthdale
heather
shooting hut
SP
grouse butts
heather
building with small arch
⑤
⑥
③
⑦
wall
barn
g/s
North Rake Hush
mine spoil
cascades and waterfalls
Slei Gill
to Tan Hill Inn
St. Mary's
LANGTHWAITE
chapel
toilets
tarmac
sewage works
②
⑧
BOOZE
g
g
g
g
g
①
to Reeth
FB
Arkle Beck

ROUTE DIRECTIONS

① From car park go R along road. In 150 yds go R over bridge and immediately turn R to follow the riverside track (BW sign). ② When track forks keep L (BW sign) uphill. From the second gate keep straight on (SP Sleigill). Ignore a footpath forking L uphill. Follow obvious green path up Slei Gill, gradually coming closer to stream on R. ③ Pass L of a building with a small arch and a few yards higher up ford a small stream. Sketchy path soon becomes clear as it swings L through heather. Path runs roughly parallel with stream and grouse butts on L, then heads for a large wooden shooting hut. ④ Go L along broad path. ⑤ When this vehicle track swings R towards a gully keep straight on up rising path to rejoin broad track as it emerges from gully. ⑥ At a track junction go L. Approaching wall fork L (marker post). ⑦ Just before reaching a barn take gate/stile (wm) in wall-corner on R. Descend field to gate at its VERY bottom. Bear L down sunken path. Near some ruins cross farm road. Continue forward down to the houses at Booze. ⑧ Return from Booze along its rough access road, which eventually acquires a tarmac surface and descends very steeply to Langthwaite.

ARKENGARTHDALE

is the Swale's major tributary valley. The fast-flowing Arkle Beck rises on the bleak moors near the famous Tan Hill Inn (England's highest pub) and flows for 11 miles to join the Swale at Grinton. The valley bottom is delightfully pastoral and well-wooded, but the upper fellsides are much scarred by the ravages of lead-mining. On the way up Slei Gill you will pass spoil heaps and a series of hushes (deep-cut gullies made by the miners of two centuries ago). The 'building with small arch' (left) is the wheel pit of one of the waterwheels which powered the mining machinery. In summer some of the spoil heaps are covered with Spring Sandwort, a starry white flower able to flourish in soil with a high lead content. Mining ended c1890.

46

A LITTLE GEM OF A WALK, IDEAL FOR A WARM SUMMER AFTERNOON OR EVENING, IN LOVELY ARKENGARTHDALE. SETTING OFF THROUGH PRETTY RIVERSIDE AND WOODLAND SCENERY, THE ROUTE THEN FOLLOWS A SUPERB GREEN TRACK UP ALONGSIDE SLEI GILL, WITH ITS CASCADES AND TINY WATERFALLS, TO LONELY HEATHER-CLAD MOORS. INTERESTING LEAD-MINING REMAINS AND, ON A CLEAR DAY, BEAUTIFUL VIEWS.

LANGTHWAITE

is the only place in Arkengarthdale of sufficient size to be classed as a village. Some of its buildings, including the Wesleyan chapel and the church, are scattered alongside the main valley road, but the hub of the village is the attractive cluster of houses huddled around the Red Lion Inn (a cosy and welcoming hostelry) on the E side of Arkle Beck.

THE CHURCH OF ST.MARY THE VIRGIN

was built in 1817 from money raised by national public subscription as a thanksgiving for the defeat of Napoleon at Waterloo. Such churches are known as 'Millions' churches, as over a million pounds was spent in this way. Strict regulations were laid down as to their form and decoration, which accounts for the church's somewhat austere appearance. The oak altar is the work of Robert Thompson, and the mouse trademark of this famous Kilburn woodcarver can be seen on top of a wall-plate on the N. wall. The churchyard has been used for several films.

Napoleon
1769-1821

unusual trough at Booze

BOOZE IS

JUST A FEW FARMS AND COTTAGES DOTTED ABOUT THE HILLSIDE AT A HEIGHT OF JUST OVER 1,000'. IT CAN HARDLY BE CALLED A HAMLET, AS IT HAS NO REAL FOCAL POINT. SADLY IT ALSO INFRINGES THE TRADES DESCRIPTIONS ACT, HAVING NEITHER PUB NOR OFF-LICENCE. STILL, NOT TO WORRY; NOT FAR NOW TO THE RED LION.

Around point 6 there are some very fine examples of BELL PITS. These indicate where early mining of lead was carried out by 'opencast' methods. Shallow shafts were dug into the vein, and the excavated soil formed a circular mound with a central depression. The ones here were probably dug in the mid-18th C.

No 9 butt

MAP O.S. Explorer OL 30 Yorkshire Dales Northern and Central areas.

47 ASKRIGG & BAINBRIDGE

5 MILES

P Askrigg. Park on the cobbles by the church (Honesty Box). Grid ref: 947 910

ROUTE DIRECTIONS

① Walk up main street. At Crown Inn take Muker road. ② Turn L (FP sign) through gate to Thorngill Cottage. Immediately take small gate (FP sign) on L. Go R through stile and ascend farm track, which soon swings L across a bridge. ③ Enter a walled lane, but immediately leave it through stile on R. Pass R of barn and climb fields, then go L along rough lane. ④ Turn L (BW Helm ½ ML) down farm road. Just before reaching farm take gate on R (between wall and fence). Keep L past wall-corner, descend to cross footbridge then forward to slit-stile in wall. ⑤ Go L along clear path which soon re-enters woodland. Follow it downhill, making a short detour sharp L (SP Mill Gill Force only) to view the waterfall. ⑥ Leave wood at a slit-stile and turn R off path. Keep bearing R up to gate/stile in wall. Cross several fields via a series of gated stiles. ⑦ Go R along road. In 80 yds take stile on L (FP Yorebridge ¼ ML). Follow partly-paved path, cross stream by a footbridge, go through remains of old railway bridge and bear R to road. ⑧ Turn L and pass through Bainbridge following Aysgarth road signs. ⑨ Turn R up lane (Semerwater, Stalling Busk) and immediately take stile on L (SP Cubeck 1½ ML). Aim for stile in wall on L, then climb to prominent slit-stile on skyline. Turn L (FP sign) alongside wall on L. Pass R of stone shed and follow clear path along edge of scar. ⑩ Fork L (FP Worton) and drop steeply to stile. Bear R to pass end of broken wall then descend to gate at far corner. Go R along road and take first L. ⑪ Cross bridge and take flagged path on L (FP Askrigg ¾). When flags end maintain direction to stile above steps. ⑫ Path turns L for 30 yds then bears R uphill to come alongside wall on L. Keep straight on between buildings then turn L to emerge opposite church.

From the farm road down to Leas House there is a superb view across Wensleydale, with the flat-topped Addlebrough very prominent.

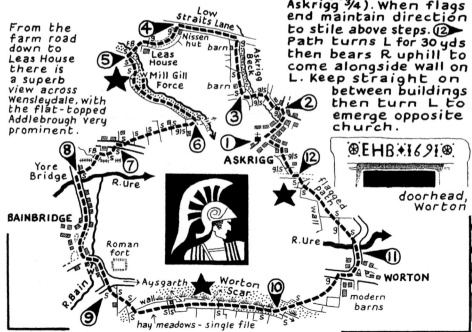

THIS SUPERB LITTLE WALK LINKS THREE CHARMING WENSLEYDALE VILLAGES AND INCLUDES A VISIT TO MILL GILL FORCE, ONE OF THE HIGHEST OF WENSLEYDALE'S MANY WATERFALLS AND MIGHTILY IMPRESSIVE AFTER HEAVY RAIN. AT PICTURESQUE BAINBRIDGE THE RIVER BAIN TUMBLES OVER A SERIES OF WIDE, ROCKY LEDGES, AND A FURTHER HIGHLIGHT IS A DELECTABLE PATH ALONG THE RIM OF A WOODED SCAR. A FEW UPS AND DOWNS BUT GENERALLY VERY EASY WALKING - IDEAL FOR A WARM SUMMER'S EVENING.

47

ASKRIGG

Morning shadows, Askrigg

A village of some size in Domesday times, Askrigg was granted a market charter in 1587, at which time it was the commercial centre of Upper Wensleydale. Many of the houses around the market place were rebuilt in three-storey fashion in the late 1700s. The large and stately Perpendicular CHURCH OF ST OSWALD dates from c1446, with restoration in c1770 and 1853. Its magnificent 16th C. wooden beamed ceiling is one of the finest in North Yorkshire. Askrigg achieved national fame through BBC TV's 'All Creatures Great and Small' series. This was where scenes for the fictitious 'Darrowby' were filmed, and the tall 'Skeldale House' opposite the church was the 'home' of vets Herriot and Farnon.

MILL GILL FORCE is a 70' waterfall plunging into an attractive wooded gorge. The woodland here is made up largely of beech, ash and sycamore, with a ground cover of ramsons (wild garlic), bluebell, dog's mercury and wood anemone.

BAINBRIDGE

is a village with a very long history. The ROMANS came here c80AD and established a FORT to the E of the R. Bain and at a crossroads on their highway network. The fort was called VIROSIDUM and was occupied for over 300 years. The site can be clearly seen in retrospect from the climb to Worton Scar. In NORMAN times Bainbridge was the HQ of the Wardens of the FOREST OF WENSLEY, a vast hunting tract. Dating from those days is the custom of Bainbridge's famous FOREST HORN, which was blown at 9 pm every winter's night between Holyrood (14 Sep) and Shrove Tuesday. 3 long blasts served to guide benighted travellers to safety. The ceremony is still carried out, and the horn can be seen in the ROSE AND CROWN, an excellent hostelry which claims to have been an inn since 1445. The STOCKS on the green are of uncertain age, but were most probably last used during the reign of ELIZABETH I (1558 - 1603).

THE BAIN IS ONE OF ENGLAND'S SHORTEST RIVERS. ITS JOURNEY FROM SEMERWATER TO THE URE BEING A MERE TWO MILES.

MICHAEL SMITH
MECHANICK
BUT HE THAT
BUILT ALL THINGS
IS GOD Heb3

inscription above window
of cottage at Worton

MAP O.S. Explorer OL 30 Yorkshire Dales Northern and Central areas.

48 CANALSIDE WALK FROM GARGRAVE

7 MILES

P Gargrave. Car park in North Street, near Village Hall. If

approaching from SE (Skipton) turn R at Old Swan Inn. If coming from W (Hellifield) turn L at Dalesman cafe.

Grid ref : 932 543

WARNING

The swans on the canal can be extremely aggressive at nesting time (April)

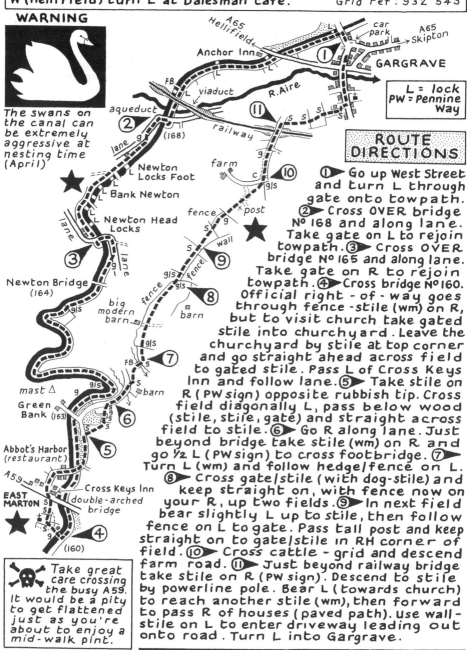

Take great care crossing the busy A59. It would be a pity to get flattened just as you're about to enjoy a mid-walk pint.

L = lock
PW = Pennine Way

ROUTE DIRECTIONS

① Go up West Street and turn L through gate onto towpath.
② Cross OVER bridge Nº 168 and along lane. Take gate on L to rejoin towpath. ③ Cross OVER bridge Nº 165 and along lane. Take gate on R to rejoin towpath. ④ Cross bridge Nº 160. Official right-of-way goes through fence-stile (wm) on R, but to visit church take gated stile into churchyard. Leave the churchyard by stile at top corner and go straight ahead across field to gated stile. Pass L of Cross Keys Inn and follow lane. ⑤ Take stile on R (PW sign) opposite rubbish tip. Cross field diagonally L, pass below wood (stile, stile, gate) and straight across field to stile. ⑥ Go R along lane. Just beyond bridge take stile (wm) on R and go ½ L (PW sign) to cross footbridge. ⑦ Turn L (wm) and follow hedge/fence on L. ⑧ Cross gate/stile (with dog-stile) and keep straight on, with fence now on your R, up two fields. ⑨ In next field bear slightly L up to stile, then follow fence on L to gate. Pass tall post and keep straight on to gate/stile in RH corner of field. ⑩ Cross cattle-grid and descend farm road. ⑪ Just beyond railway bridge take stile on R (PW sign). Descend to stile by powerline pole. Bear L (towards church) to reach another stile (wm), then forward to pass R of houses (paved path). Use wall-stile on L to enter driveway leading out onto road. Turn L into Gargrave.

AND NOW FOR SOMETHING COMPLETELY DIFFERENT..... A 4 MILE STROLL ALONG THE TOWPATH OF THE LEEDS - LIVERPOOL CANAL, WITH A RETURN TO GARGRAVE THROUGH THE LUSH GREEN PASTURES OF ONE OF THE MOST RURAL SECTIONS OF THE PENNINE WAY. VERY EASY WALKING, WITH A PUB (CROSS KEYS) AND TEA SHOP (ABBOT'S HARBOR) AT THE HALF-WAY POINT. BE SURE TO DO THE WALK IN HIGH SUMMER, WHEN THE CANAL IS THRONGED WITH COLOURFUL HOLIDAY CRAFT.

48

THE
LEEDS & LIVERPOOL
CANAL

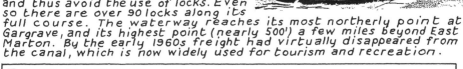

At 127 miles this is Britain's longest canal. Its construction was authorised by Parliament in 1770, and the first length to be completed – from Bingley to Skipton – was opened in 1773. The complete canal was finally opened in 1816, and had cost £1¼ million. Notice how, between Newton Bridge and East Marton, the canal makes big sweeping bends in order to contour the land and thus avoid the use of locks. Even so there are over 90 locks along its full course. The waterway reaches its most northerly point at Gargrave, and its highest point (nearly 500') a few miles beyond East Marton. By the early 1960s freight had virtually disappeared from the canal, which is now widely used for tourism and recreation.

St. Peter's — E. Marton

EAST MARTON St. Peter's Church dates back to c 1147. Its sturdy Norman tower has, on its S wall, a sundial dated 1714. The interior has much of interest, including an unusual 17th C. ceiling, a couple of ancient box pews and a Norman font.

GARGRAVE IS A LARGE AND THRIVING VILLAGE SPLIT BY THE VERY BUSY A65. THE CHURCH OF ST. ANDREW WAS REBUILT IN THE MID-19TH C., BUT RETAINS ITS PERPENDICULAR TOWER (1521) AND HAS SOME BEAUTIFUL STAINED GLASS. THE E WINDOW HAS AN UNUSUAL CRUCIFIXION SCENE DEPICTING THE THIEVES, THE WOMEN AND ST. JOHN. THE PULPIT WAS RESTORED IN MEMORY OF CHARLES MARSDEN, WHO WAS VICAR HERE FOR 57 YEARS. HIGH STREET HAS A WIDE ENOUGH RANGE OF SHOPS TO PROVIDE SOME RETAIL THERAPY. NORTH STREET HAS A ROW OF 17TH C. COTTAGES, AND OPPOSITE IS STORY'S HOUSE, BUILT IN 1828 BY ROBERT STORY, SCHOOLMASTER AND POET.

MAP O.S. Explorer OL 2 Yorkshire Dales Southern and Western areas.

49 KINGSDALE

6 MILES

ROUTE DIRECTIONS ①

P Twisleton Lane, a rough track which joins the Thornton in Lonsdale – Dent road about 1½ miles N of Thornton. Space for a few vehicles on the grass verge. BE SURE NOT TO OBSTRUCT ACCESS. *Grid ref: 692 760*

Walk along road towards Thornton. In 60yds take ladder-stile on R (FP Turbary rd ¾ ML) and climb to ladder-stile on skyline. Climb next low scar, turn R to wall and climb alongside it. ② ▶ At wall-corner turn R and follow broad track (Turbary Road), passing huge rift of Rowten Pot (see notes on next page). ③ ▶ Short detour L to visit Jingling Pot (marked by tree). ④ ▶ A few yds beyond a gate (just before track swings L uphill) you'll see a small patch of outcrops on your R. Make towards LH side of these to locate thin path running level along hillside to Bull Pot (marked by small hawthorn). Turn R down towards trees and go R along rim of scar to a point where its safe and easy to descend. Cross field to roadside gate. ⑤ ▶ Go L along road. Take next gate on L and climb to Yordas Cave. Retrace steps to point 5 and continue along road. ⑥ ▶ Take ladder-stile on L (FP Scar End 1¾). Cross footbridge and head towards LH end of wood. Cross wall-stile (FP sign) at top of small hillock. At far end of long wooden barn turn L up to house. Take gate on R (FP sign) and turn L to stile. ⑦ ▶ Go straight on, keeping parallel with wood, to ladder-stile at its far end. ⑧ ▶ Bear L uphill to ladder-stile in crosswall. Follow thin path alongside wall, then fence, on R. On nearing a crosswall the path climbs L to a ladder-stile. ⑨ ▶ Follow thin, winding path, with fence on L, to wall-stile. Continue forward to ladder-stile. ⑩ ▶ Forward for about 200yds (green path) then turn sharp R down grassy slope to rough lane. Follow it R to car.

On summer weekends there's often an ice-cream van on Twisleton Lane.

Dent

Yordas Cave

Bull Pot

Shout Scar

motor road

Jingling Pot and Cave

Rowten Caves

FB Kingsdale Beck (dry bed)

boggy × trough

wall

Rowten Pot (see notes on next page)

slopes of Gragareth

Turbary Pot

High Plain

no path

Braida Garth

kiln

Turbary Road

wall

Blea Dubs

Kail Pot

KINGSDALE

Botany Bay

fence   wall   wall

thin path

George's Scar

Low Plain

Kingsdale Beck

Cheese Press Stone

clints and boulders

Wackenburgh Hill

fence

Thornton in Lonsdale

FB

path to Thornton Force

Twisleton Scar End

Twisleton Lane

108

WILD AND LONELY KINGSDALE IS A GEOLOGICAL CLASSIC - A STRAIGHT, GLACIATED TROUGH THOUGHT TO HAVE ONCE CONTAINED A LAKE. ITS SIDES ARE LINED WITH LIMESTONE SCARS RIDDLED WITH CAVES AND POTHOLES, AND SOME OF THE MOST NOTABLE OF THESE ARE VISITED ON THE WALK ALONG THE TURBARY ROAD, A GREEN, HIGH-LEVEL TRACK RUNNING ALONG A NATURAL LIMESTONE SHELF. ALL THE EXCITING BITS OCCUR ON THIS SECTION, AS FAR AS YORDAS CAVE. THE INITIAL CLIMB IS VERY ROUGH UNDERFOOT IN PLACES ; ALL THE REST IS EASY GOING. Note : Yordas Cave floods after heavy rain.

49

The Cheese Press Stone

These boulders were probably deposited here by a retreating glacier. The larger block is 9' high and weighs 15 tons.

KAIL POT is a wide and impressive 33' shaft a few yards down to the R of the track.

TURBARY POT, in a small rocky shakehole immediately L of the track, is a 16' deep rift leading to a 115' shaft.

ROWTEN POT

A hole by the side of the track, where the roof of Rowten Cave has collapsed, reveals the stream flowing into nearby Rowten Pot.

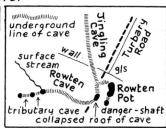

underground line of cave
surface stream
wall
Jingling Cave
Turbary Road
gls
Rowten Cave
Rowten Pot
tributary cave / danger-shaft
collapsed roof of cave

Turn L off the track here and in 100yds across the moor you will find the cave entrance, where the stream disappears underground. 30yds to the R of the stream sink is another cave containing a tiny tributary stream, and a trip through this is easy and interesting. Return to Rowten Pot, a huge and dangerous chasm descending to a depth of some 350'. A smaller hole a few yards to the S is even more dangerous, being the top of a 220' straight shaft.

At **JINGLING POT** a rowan overhangs a 140' shaft. Nearby a stream flows into a cave en route for Rowten Pot ● **BULL POT** is a 40' deep rift covered with rusty iron sheeting.

Rowten Cave - stream entrance.

YORDAS CAVE

In Victorian times this was a show cave. To explore it you will need a powerful and reliable torch. From the entrance – a low stone-built arch at the base of a rock wall – a few steps lead down to a floor of firm mud. Beware of low-hanging rocks. Go forward, following the RH wall into the huge main chamber - 180' long, 50' wide and 70' high. A shallow stream flows over gravel and pebbles. Turn R, following the sound of water, to head for the top LH corner, and here step through rock arches to view a waterfall plunging down a high circular shaft known as 'The Chapter House'.

If your energy knows no bounds, you could tag on the famous and spectacular INGLETON WATERFALLS WALK by keeping straight ahead from point 10 along Twisleton Lane. The route is obvious – no map or guidebook necessary. This would make a walk of 10 miles ; too much these days for your venerable author, but if you're fit enough go for it. **NOTE**: You'll have to pay an admission fee at the official entrance half-way round.

MAP O.S. Explorer OL 2 Yorkshire Dales Southern and Western areas.

50 THREE VILLAGES OF COVERDALE

P Horsehouse.
There is roadside space for 3 or 4 cars at N end of village opposite the end of a lane with a 'No Through Road' sign.
Grid ref: 047 813

ROUTE DIRECTIONS ① Start along rough lane behind Thwaite Arms. At FP sign turn R down through 2 gates then go L (FP Gammersgill 1) to gate (wm). Pass below barn to reach river at a footbridge, but DON'T CROSS IT. Follow riverside path through several stiles. ② From stile by powerline pole head L towards farmhouse. Cross wall-stile 60 yds to its R and go forward through trees. Turn R along road. ③ Take stile on R (FP Carlton 1¼). Bear L to wall-stile and forward along an enclosed path to footbridge. ④ Turn R to stile (wm) at wall-corner and maintain a level course. Cross tiny stream then 3 stiles. Turn L up road. ⑤ Take stile on R (FP Carlton ½). Forward through another stile then bear L to stile in corner. Climb field to gate near prominent mound. Follow road all the way through the village. ⑥ Turn R down Quaker Lane (SP River Cover, West Scrafton). At its end take gate on R and follow RH edge of field. Go through gate and follow fence L. Descend steeply to cross two footbridges. ⑦ Climb alongside trees to gate, bear R up to SP, then cut back L to gate/ladder-stile. Keep close to gill – DON'T cross bridge – to reach stile, then climb bank and follow lane into village. ⑧ Turn R along road and in 50 yds fork L up tarmac lane to Swineside. ⑨ At hamlet keep L of all buildings to gate/stile. Maintain level course cont. R

CARLTON

Quaker's Garth

Goodman's Gill

helluva tight squeeze

R. Cover

Caygill Scar (ravine) ⑦ ★

WEST SCRAFTON

road

Bow Bridge ⑧

Westclose House

R. Cover

tarmac lane

The prominent outcrop on the L skyline is Great Roova Crags

Gammersgill ③

gls ruin

② Coverdale Country Hotel

barn

barn

Swineside

gls ⑨

Rampshaw Bank
rabbit warren

wall

stone bridge

gls

⑩

★

ROUTE DIRECTIONS cont: through several broken walls. ⑩ From gated stile in crosswall go ½ R (FP sign) down to stile. Maintain direction (FP sign) to cross tiny stream then keep a level course to cross another. Bear R to pass (via stiles) through young plantation. ⑪ Head for farm. Take gated stile to its R. Cross footbridge to re-join outward route.

P barn
MP

⑪ Hindlethwaite Hall

HORSEHOUSE ①

THIS GENTLE, LOW-LEVEL WALK GIVES AN OPPORTUNITY TO APPRAISE THE CONSIDERABLE CHARM OF PEACEFUL COVERDALE, ONE OF THE LEAST-VISITED OF THE MAJOR DALES. EN ROUTE WE VISIT THE THREE PRINCIPAL VILLAGES OF THIS SPARSELY POPULATED VALLEY, HORSEHOUSE, CARLTON AND WEST SCRAFTON, WITH A COUPLE OF HAMLETS (GAMMERSGILL AND SWINESIDE) THROWN IN FOR GOOD MEASURE. THERE ARE MANY INTERESTING AND ATTRACTIVE OLD BUILDINGS ALONG THE WAY. NOT THE BEST OF DOGGY WALKS — COWS AND SHEEP ALL OVER THE PLACE.

50

COVERDALE

is the longest of Wensleydale's many side-valleys. From its rising on the slopes of Great Whernside the River Cover flows for some 15 miles to join the Ure just below Middleham. A famous son of the dale was Miles Coverdale, Bishop of Exeter, who undertook the first translation of the Bible into English - a task he completed in 1535.

MILES COVERDALE 1488-1568

HORSEHOUSE

St. Botolph's, Horsehouse

The hoary old grey buildings of this tiny village cluster haphazardly around a cosy pub (Thwaite Arms) and a modest little church. The name 'Horsehouse' suggests that this was a resting place for pack-horses travelling between Wharfedale and Middleham. St. Botolph's Church was established c1530 as a chapel-of-ease run by the monks of Coverham Abbey. It was rebuilt in 1869, but the window at the base of the tower is thought to be original. The churchyard has a very old and rare Weeping Beech tree.

ST. BOTOLPH, ACCORDING TO THE ANGLO-SAXON CHRONICLE, WAS THE FOUNDER AND FIRST ABBOT OF A MONASTERY AT ICANHOE IN 645, BUT IT IS UNCERTAIN WHETHER THIS WAS AT IKEN (SUFFOLK) OR BOSTON (LINCS), WHERE THE PARISH CHURCH – THE FAMOUS BOSTON STUMP – IS ONE OF SOME 70 ENGLISH CHURCHES DEDICATED TO THIS RATHER OBSCURE SAINT. ST. BOTOLPH'S DAY IS THE 17TH JUNE.

This old caravan has nestled snugly under its archway at Gammersgill for donkey's years, and has become a familiar landmark for motorists driving up the dale.

CARLTON

is by far the largest village in Coverdale, and its many fine houses are indicative of its prosperity in the 17th and 18th centuries. One house has an inscribed tablet stating that this was the home of Henry Constantine (a local dialect poet known as 'The Coverdale Bard'). Before leaving the village you may care to wet your whistle at the excellent Foresters Arms.

The houses of **WEST SCRAFTON** are closely grouped around a tiny green. The large house near the telephone box was once the Moorhen Inn. There is no public access to the ravine, which is a pity, for it's a fine limestone gorge with a cave – Tom Hunter's Parlour – said to be named after a local highwayman.

'Hindlethwaite' means 'forest clearing for hinds' (female deer).

MAP O.S. Explorer OL 30 Yorkshire Dales Northern and Central areas.

Thankyou Lord
  For the beauty of the Yorkshire Dales,
  For the fun and friendship of holidays,
  For the leisure to rest, sleep and eat.
Help us Lord to see your work
            in the beauty of creation;
To know your presence in the jumble of our lives;
To share your love
            in the depths of our relationships.
      For Jesus sake
            Amen

FROM ST. MARGARET'S CHURCH, HAWES
ADAPTED FROM A PRAYER BY CHRISTOPHER CHAPMAN

THE WALKS - A PERSONAL RECORD

1	MARSKE BECK			
DATE	START	FINISH	MARKS	
(Notes – Weather, Companions, Highlights, Disasters etc)	(Times)		(Out of 10)	

2	CAVES AND GORGES OF NIDDERDALE			
DATE	START	FINISH	MARKS	

3	CONISTONE DIB AND DIB SCAR			
DATE	START	FINISH	MARKS	

4	PENYGHENT			
DATE	START	FINISH	MARKS	

5	LANGSTROTHDALE			
DATE	START	FINISH	MARKS	

6	KISDON AND THE SWALE GORGE			
DATE	START	FINISH	MARKS	

7	EAVESTON LAKE			
DATE	START	FINISH	MARKS	

8	SWINSTY AND FEWSTON			
DATE	START	FINISH	MARKS	

9	FROSTROW FELLS			
DATE	START	FINISH	MARKS	

10	HARDRAW FORCE			
DATE	START	FINISH	MARKS	

11	GUNNERSIDE GILL			
DATE	START	FINISH	MARKS	

12	MAGICAL MALHAM			
DATE	START	FINISH	MARKS	

13	PENYGHENT GILL			
DATE	START	FINISH	MARKS	

14	CRUMMACK DALE			
DATE	START	FINISH	MARKS	

15	ILKLEY MOOR			
DATE	START	FINISH	MARKS	

16	HARD LEVEL GILL			
DATE	START	FINISH	MARKS	

17	JERVAULX ABBEY			
DATE	START	FINISH	MARKS	

18	AYSGARTH AND WEST BURTON			
DATE	START	FINISH	MARKS	

19	TROLLERS GILL			
DATE	START	FINISH	MARKS	

20	GAPING GILL			
DATE	START	FINISH	MARKS	

21	SETTLE AND CLEATOP PARK			
DATE	START	FINISH	MARKS	

22	PATELEY BRIDGE AND WATH			
DATE	START	FINISH	MARKS	

23	OLD COTE MOOR AND LITTONDALE			
DATE	START	FINISH	MARKS	

24	INGLEBOROUGH			
DATE	START	FINISH	MARKS	

25	FLASBY FELL			
DATE	START	FINISH	MARKS	

26	SEMER WATER			
DATE	START	FINISH	MARKS	

27	MARRICK PRIORY			
DATE	START	FINISH	MARKS	

28 THE DRUID'S TEMPLE

DATE	START	FINISH	MARKS	

29 SIMON'S SEAT

DATE	START	FINISH	MARKS	

30 PENHILL

DATE	START	FINISH	MARKS	

31 CAVES AND POTHOLES OF BIRKWITH

DATE	START	FINISH	MARKS	

32 CATRIGG FORCE AND VICTORIA CAVE

DATE	START	FINISH	MARKS	

33 WILLANCE'S LEAP

DATE	START	FINISH	MARKS	

34 HACK FALL

DATE	START	FINISH	MARKS	

35	CAPPLESTONE GATE			
DATE		START	FINISH	MARKS

36	FEIZOR			
DATE		START	FINISH	MARKS

37	COTTERDALE			
DATE		START	FINISH	MARKS

38	DALLOWGILL			
DATE		START	FINISH	MARKS

39	MUKER AND OXNOP			
DATE		START	FINISH	MARKS

40	BRIMHAM ROCKS			
DATE		START	FINISH	MARKS

41	BORDLEY TOWN			
DATE		START	FINISH	MARKS

42	WHERNSIDE		
DATE	START	FINISH	MARKS

43	LOWER COVERDALE		
DATE	START	FINISH	MARKS

44	BEYOND MALHAM TARN		
DATE	START	FINISH	MARKS

45	BUCKDEN PIKE		
DATE	START	FINISH	MARKS

46	BOOZE		
DATE	START	FINISH	MARKS

47	ASKRIGG AND BAINBRIDGE		
DATE	START	FINISH	MARKS

48	CANALSIDE WALK FROM GARGRAVE		
DATE	START	FINISH	MARKS

49	**KINGSDALE**				
DATE	START	FINISH	MARKS	

50	**THREE VILLAGES OF COVERDALE**				
DATE	START	FINISH	MARKS	

 # NATIONAL PARK CENTRES

AYSGARTH FALLS
Tel: 01969 662910
Fax: 01969 662929
E-mail: aysgarth@yorkshiredales.org.uk

GRASSINGTON
Tel: 01756 751690
Fax: 01756 751693
E-mail: grassington@yorkshiredales.org.uk

HAWES
Tel: 01969 666210
Fax: 01969 666239
E-mail: hawes@yorkshiredales.org.uk

MALHAM
Tel: 01969 652380
Fax: 01969 652389
E-mail: malham@yorkshiredales.org.uk

REETH
Tel: 01748 884059
Fax: 01748 880012
E-mail: reeth@yorkshiredales.org.uk